THE EMERALD GUIDE TO ANN OAKLEY

Emerald Guides to Social Thought

Series Editor: John Scott

Emerald Guides to Social Thought are a series of student-oriented guides to major thinkers on social issues.

Each book is an authoritative primer that takes the reader through the key ideas of a thinker in order to provide a firm foundation for an independent reading of primary texts, for engagement with the secondary literature, and for reading contemporary extensions and elaborations of those ideas. The Guides demonstrate the mind of the theorist at work by tracing the development of that thought through successive texts or by elucidating the various topics to which they have been applied.

Emerald Guides place the work of a thinker in the context of her or his life and times. Substantive and comprehensive chapters on key issues are followed by full guides to sources of information and translation that provide a clear 'map' of the thinker's intellectual development, and to major items of commentary, debate, and application of their ideas.

The Guides are uniquely authoritative and accessible and provide the foundations of a scholarly library that allow the reader to develop his or her own ideas regarding influential thinkers and theorists.

THE EMERALD GUIDE TO ANN OAKLEY

BY

GRAHAM CROW
University of Edinburgh, UK

United Kingdom – North America – Japan – India
Malaysia – China

Emerald Publishing Limited
Emerald Publishing, Floor 5, Northspring, 21-23 Wellington Street,
Leeds LS1 4DL

First edition 2024

British Library Cataloguing in Publication Data
A catalogue record for this book is available from the British Library

ISBN: 978-1-80071-564-6 (Print)
ISBN: 978-1-80071-561-5 (Online)
ISBN: 978-1-80071-563-9 (Epub)

INVESTOR IN PEOPLE

'To Joyce, my mother'

CONTENTS

ABOUT THE AUTHOR

Graham Crow is an Emeritus Professor of Sociology and Methodology at the University of Edinburgh. During his career, he held the posts of Director of the Scottish Graduate School of Social Science and Deputy Director of the National Centre for Research Methods. His interests include the sociology of family and community, sociological theory, comparative sociology, research methodology and academic careers and retirement. In 2021, he was awarded the British Sociological Association Distinguished Service Award.

ACKNOWLEDGEMENTS

I would like to thank Gillian Bendelow, Karen Dunnell, Ros Edwards, Ruben Flores, Ann Oakley, John Scott and Rose Wiles for their very helpful comments on an earlier draft of this book. Any errors or other shortcomings remain my responsibility, of course.

1

ANN OAKLEY'S IDEAS IN CONTEXT

Ann Oakley's career began against the backdrop of 1960s radicalism. This decade saw growing disquiet regarding women's inferior status to men in both the public and private spheres which prompted far-reaching reconsideration of what it meant to be a wife, a mother, a woman and a citizen. Oakley was able to bring newly acquired personal experience to bear on such issues through reaching adulthood, marrying, bearing children and starting out as a researcher during these turbulent years. Questioning the extent to which unequal social, economic and political outcomes for women and men could be explained by sex differences led her to develop the distinction between sex and gender in her path-breaking first book, written at pace while she was still studying for her PhD on the sociology of housework. The policy of the Social Science Research Council (the funding council which supported her doctoral research) of paying a lower stipend to married women on the grounds that their husbands were partially responsible for their upkeep brought home the banality of everyday inequality between women and men, as did the commonplace expression of being 'just' a housewife as an indication of lower standing. The study of sociology expanded rapidly in the United Kingdom in the 1960s, but its then mainstream view emphasised the powerful forces of social-isation moulding people for distinctive sex roles that were supposedly functional for the wider social system. By contrast, dissident voices portrayed marriage and the family as sites of oppression which people were conditioned (even brain-washed) to accept. Contestation of wider ideas about mas-culinity and femininity and their related mystiques followed. Feminist investigations revealed how mainstream thinking turned out to be 'malestream' (that is, embedded in a set of assumptions containing systematic biases against women). This opened up avenues of enquiry that continue to rever-berate more than half a century later.

Oakley took readily to debating inequalities between the sexes and gender politics more generally and was already cultivating her capacity to approach these issues from sur-prising angles. The work of her father, the eminent Professor of Social Administration at the London School of Economics (LSE) Richard Titmuss, included studies of the implications for social policy of the changing position of women. These may have been among those of his writings that she as a teenager helped him to prepare for publication (for example, by checking referencing, about which, she later recalled, he was not always scrupulous). Her father's academic colleagues to whom she was introduced included Barbara Wootton, whose elevation to the House of Lords enabled her to do something about the sex discrimination her research had highlighted, as Oakley observed in the biography of the Baroness that she would later write. As an undergraduate at the University of Oxford, Oakley criticised the sociology of the family that she encountered, considering its male authors complacent. She was, however, enthused by Charles Wright Mills's arguments regarding the sociological imagination and his way of envisaging how social arrangements could be radically different and, moreover, written about accessibly. Her direct experience of marriage, motherhood and housework confirmed her sense of the discordance between idealised portrayals and mundane realities, and this motivated her to challenge prevailing myths. From the outset, her research deployed the simple but effective technique of directing attention to disconcerting truths, such as pointing out the number of hours spent on housework, or the unsustainable combination of biological and social constructionist elements in the concept of sex roles. Feminism has the capacity to shock people who hold common sense points of view, and Oakley used this to challenge women's subordinate position and to make the case against sexism, furthering the broader endeavour of taking women seriously in a man's world.

Second wave feminism's revitalisation of the women's movement emphasised the collective, sisterly nature of contesting male domination and masculine norms. Much would have remained hidden without the myriad contributions to the common cause of questioning and seeking to replace hidebound social arrangements which defined women through their relationship to men. An important first step was to identify the issues that confronted women. Betty Friedan's best-selling 1963 book *The Feminine Mystique* described women's sense of unease at their situation, designating it a problem that had no name. This opened the way to the discovery, sometimes via rediscovery, of the reasons for women's lack of recognition or appreciation in social life and for the disproportionate attention paid to men in supposedly scientific accounts of how society operates. Women's invisibility was exemplified by housework and its treatment as something other than work, something secondary to the main event of employment and thus a trivial concern. Earlier generations of women writers (including Wootton) had reflected on the conundrum of housework being unpaid when undertaken by a family member but paid when performed as a service, and contesting this double standard was central to the 1970s campaign for wages for housework. On a more theoretical level, participants in the domestic labour debate sought to grasp the relationship between housework and capitalism, although not all feminists shared this preoccupation. The different visions of socialist, radical and other strands of feminist thinking reflected the wide range of perspectives available between whose adherents vigorous dialogues took place, including with regard to who or what constituted 'the main enemy' of the Women's Liberation Movement. These debates were sometimes conducted more brusquely than was Oakley's preference, mirroring rather than escaping the combative academic conventions from which she also felt alienated.

Feminist perspectives directed attention to a host of previously-neglected topics besides housework that were central to women's lives including everyday harassment, domestic violence, household budgeting, food, emotions, and childbirth. Childbirth and motherhood provided the subject matter for Oakley's next major project and followed her housework study's use of interview material to allow women's voices more of a hearing. These accounts of becoming a mother contradicted the prevailing viewpoints and practices of the medical professionals who controlled the process of human reproduction, thereby challenging their professional expertise. Oakley's own experience while pregnant of service provision being male-dominated was consistent with not only the numerical preponderance of male obstetricians but also their practice of treating women's bodies as machines that had developed a fault and needed repair. By contrast, midwives were predominantly women who approached maternity as a normal occurrence and whose history of practice was less medicalised. The reassertion of the case for female control of childbirth had both direct practical implications and consequences for theoretical analyses about the nature and purpose of knowledge and its production, dissemination and contestation in patriarchal societies. Ensuing debates extended to consideration of the methodological foundations of knowledge claims and counter claims about such issues. These encounters could be abrasive, as the use of the term 'paradigm wars' to describe them indicates. To many in the anti-positivist camp Oakley's qualitative research appeared to provide support for their position in this long-running conflict, but her endorsement of quantitative methods (and, in particular, randomised controlled trials) reduced her partisan appeal. Opinions vary on how long the paradigm wars lasted, but when eventually they were succeeded by a more tolerant and pluralistic détente Oakley could feel vindicated regarding the positions she had adopted.

Oakley's work is characterised by preparedness to experiment with various presentational formats. Mindful of the need of the growing numbers of students on women's studies courses for an accessible textbook she wrote one that she considered might also profitably be read by men. Her commitment to put into practice the ambition of reaching general as well as academic audiences for her research led to appearances on popular radio and television programmes, to writing for mass-circulation magazines and to weaving her ideas into further literary forms, such as novels, poetry and autobiography. Deploying means of revealing the nature of the world other than those associated with conventional scientific modes of publication has a long history that was reinvigorated by the intellectual trend known as post-modernism. The demolition of the much-vaunted Pruitt-Igoe public housing scheme in the USA in 1972 represented a key moment of disenchantment with modernist thinking that extended beyond the failure of architectural projects into numerous practical fields from penal policy to economic development strategies. The critique of professional expertise that post-modernists advanced along with their objections to the deployment of binary oppositions and their openness to being playful with form bore points of connection to Oakley's work. She was, however, unconvinced by post-modernists' relativism and their scepticism regarding attempts to influence policy-makers in the pursuit of securing improvements in people's lives, that is, to academics making a practical difference. Moreover, post-modernist thinking posed a fundamental challenge to many feminists by problematising the core category of women. Although not everyone agreed with Oakley's description of post-modernism as delusional or suicidal, she was far from alone in doubting post-modernists' capacity to confront political challenges effectively. This issue's importance was crystallised by a sustained backlash against feminism, with various forces seeking to prevent further progress, if not to reverse altogether the gains made by the women's movement.

Oakley did criticise science and scientists on several grounds, such as their predisposition to treat hysteria as a condition to which women were uniquely vulnerable, and related gender biases embodied in their starting assumptions. She was, however, also keen to acknowledge and promote the value of rigorous scientific endeavour. In the context of the backlash against feminism, and of welfare state retrenchment and social polarisation, she highlighted the need for systematic evidence concerning the extent to which moves towards greater gender equality had been achieved or frustrated. The direction of travel of Oakley's career in the 1980s was towards policy-relevant research, and the establishment in 1990 of the Social Science Research Unit with her as Director (followed shortly after by being made Professor of Sociology and Social Policy) facilitated her pursuit of practical feminism in other fields besides health such as education, social work and relationships within families. Systematic reviewing of evidence was central to this agenda because without it the elementary goal of knowledge being cumulative is much harder to achieve. In particular, systematic reviews allow proper assessments to be made of policy interventions; initiatives do not always have the impact intended, and on occasion they have the opposite effect. Systematic reviewing represented for Oakley the opportunity for sociologists to move beyond finding what they hoped or expected to find. It required them to think more rigorously about research design and data analysis, although treating it as a giant leap for the discipline may yet turn out to have been premature. In terms of her own trajectory it was less of a revolutionary change than a natural progression from her earlier work, although some people were surprised by it. In her view, methodological choices should be determined by the appropriateness of the tools to the task in hand, not by the slavish adherence to only one approach which Alvin Gouldner termed methodolatry.

The significance of research context was highlighted when Oakley returned to investigating the process of becoming a mother as both a re-study and a follow-up study more than three decades on from her original project. This required paying attention to changes in the circumstances in which women became mothers but also to continuities. Mothers in the new century came from a more diverse set of households and were typically older than their 1970s counterparts; they were also much more likely to have Caesarean births and to be discharged from hospital more rapidly. Despite these changes, and the need to update some questions' wording, many of the original study's findings about motherhood, including its travails, continued to apply. Similar opportunities for taking stock of developments had presented themselves when writing introductions to new

editions of books and other published material. Fresh generations of readers needed to be provided with background information about the intellectual, political and personal contexts in
which the original outputs had been produced, and the things
that Oakley needed to explain expanded as the time distance
from the originals' publication dates grew. Her earlier work may
have been open to criticism from her later self as at times naïve or
suffering from other shortcomings, but it deserved to be judged
as a product of its time. Some of the positions and language
adopted several decades previously have, unsurprisingly, come
to seem anachronistic, or alternatively commonplace and
unremarkable for those ideas that have permeated mainstream
thinking. Reflections on earlier work understandably prompt
researchers to consider the nature and direction of their career
trajectories. In Oakley's case this extended to considering the
seriousness of the obstacles encountered that made it difficult to
plan ahead, especially around combining motherhood and paid
work, even more so where that paid work took the form of a
succession of short-term contracts. She reflected on how this and
the serendipity involved in moving from one project to another
make it inappropriate to treat her achievements as constituting a
career, at least in the conventional sense of that term. Other
people's accounts of apparently effortless career progression
may be plausible, but in many cases the suspicion remains of
sanitisation of the record to support a comforting fable, or a
hagiographic legend.

The obstacles to women's career opportunities and ways of
overcoming them represent long-standing concerns for feminists.
Oakley has engaged with this important issue at various points.
Her study of housework led to critical reflections on women's
invisibility to (or at least inadequate representation by) the
mainstream sociologists of the time who took their lead from the
so-called founding fathers of the discipline. Karl Marx, Émile
Durkheim, Max Weber and others stood charged not only with

academic sexism but also with domestic oppression of their wives and daughters through conventional household arrangements that freed up their time to write. Second wave feminists wondered how much had changed in the interim, although their efforts within the British Sociological Association (BSA) initiated a powerful challenge to male hegemony in terms of working practices. By the late 20th century, the BSA's gender ratios had shifted dramatically so that women comprised the majority of members based at UK universities though not of university-based sociologists overall. Furthermore, inequality in pay, security and prestige remained significant. Oakley returned to the theme of academic sexism in a series of book projects based on archival research into the lives of women whose contributions had not received due recognition during their lifetimes and were neglected after their deaths. Barbara Wootton's profile as an academic and political figure merited particular attention. She helped to found the BSA, served as its first President, and had a remarkable record of achievement in public life as well as academically, but by the time of Oakley's biography she was largely unremembered and unacknowledged. In an earlier era the same fate had befallen the hundreds of first-wave feminists who had been active during the 40 years from 1880 who were the subjects of *Women, Peace and Welfare*, Oakley's later book which traced their suppressed history. A further publication in this vein, *Forgotten Wives*, told the story of the spouses of four men whose achievements as public figures continue to be celebrated, but with scant appreciation of their partners' roles in bringing about those achievements.

Writing biographies involves consideration of what to include about a person's life and what to omit in telling their story in a way that is respectful to the people concerned and intelligible and engaging to readers. The same consideration applies to autobiographical accounts. The feminist slogan 'the personal is political' contested the idea that attention should focus exclusively on the public realm; understanding the private sphere is a necessary part of appreciating not only how gender inequalities are reproduced but also the broader question of how people's identities are shaped, and in some situations eroded. The key sociological interests in making connections between personal troubles and public issues and between an individual's biography and historical trends encourage consideration of the influences that mould us. Oakley appreciated on a personal level the tension between who a person is and what they are supposed to be. She came to recognise that these unsettling existential questions of self and purpose, concerning the gap between expectation and reality and the related experience of feeling bad while doing good, were part of what the social forces of the 1960s (including feminism's challenge to inherited ideas) had helped to create. Her heartfelt account of how interviewing in the manner in which she had been taught turned out to be both impractical and unethical unexpectedly struck a chord with fellow researchers who have cited it more than any other of her publications. Further aspects of her writing that shares what her life experiences have taught her about herself have proved recognisable to many readers. Alongside the unique aspects of every individual's life, there are similarities to and points of connection with the lived experiences of others. These might, for example, relate to Oakley's accounts of her position as an outsider, her shyness, her ambivalent feelings about family relationships, or her encounters with illness, including ones that are taboo. Writing plainly about such subjects does not necessarily make for easy reading, but telling the truth is a surer path to liberation than pretence or self-deception.

A person does not have to be typical of wider populations for their experiences to resonate with others. Early second-wave feminists like Oakley have nevertheless had to confront the issue of how their whiteness and middle-class status sets their situation apart from that of women of different ethnicities and social classes, with further contrasts relating to disability, sexuality, age and generation, household type and the global fissure between North and South. These variations in degrees of disempowerment undoubtedly complicate the category of women, but they do not obviate the need for it all the while that gender persists as a common basis of marginalisation in a world built by men around masculine norms. The idea that biology does not ineluctably determine a person's destiny remains a powerful rationale for feminism in the context of women's position being systematically inferior to men's. In response to the backlash against the women's movement, Oakley continued to echo Simone de Beauvoir's telling phrase that women are not born but made. This element of Oakley's work confronted and engaged with the arguments of the backlash rather than simply dismissing them, recognising that they had achieved some pur-chase with members of younger generations who were persuaded (wrongly, in Oakley's view) that the need for femi-nism had become less pressing. Besides updating the evidence of enduring gendered inequality in some fields alongside progress in others, her case extended beyond restatement of the initial position in further ways by discussing developments in biology (in particular, genetics) and gender crossing. Disputing the deep-rooted belief that women can be reduced to their bodies requires understanding not only of its long history but also of its latest incarnations.

The use of a particular instance of gender crossing (that told by the economist Deirdre McCloskey of her transition from being Donald) in Oakley's discussion of the subject in *Gender on Planet Earth* reveals her preference for the greater ease with which the story of an individual life can be grasped, compared to the generalities of abstract theories. The concept of patriarchy does inform her work, but it is used sparingly. In part this is because such phenomena are hard to grasp (thereby presenting a challenge to writers whose ambitions include accessibility to a broad range of readers), but it also reflects a preference for working in a bottom-up fashion, rather than starting with theory, grand or otherwise. Oakley was led to feminism in no small part by becoming a mother, and many of her research questions have been grounded in her own experiences or those of women known to her. Finding that housewifely duties like cleaning the lavatory were inadequately accounted for by a theory that allocated so-called expressive roles to women on the grounds of their sex meant that a new theory urgently needed to be developed. The concept of gender that Oakley advanced early in her career to allow women to have selves that were distinct from their bodies has served her well over several decades, although the proliferation of the term's usage and the academic and political contestation that have accompanied it necessarily complicate matters. Oakley's contribution is not always explicitly acknowledged by those striving to make gender progressively less significant as a feature of social organisation, but the durability of gender inequalities suggests that she and her collaborators merit inclusion in accounts of what one such collaborator, Juliet Mitchell, called the longest revolution.

In the discussion of ideas and of the people whose careers are forged through working with them, there are elements of circularity alongside claims to progress. Oakley is aware that her career has taken her, via circuitous routes, to new versions of her starting points with the study of housework and the concept of gender. She was also aware of repetitive elements in debates about women's employment. Pearl Jephcott's investigation (with which Oakley's father had a role) into married women's employment used an innovative methodological repertoire to explain why married women were increasingly taking up paid work, in the process challenging once again the dubious association of working mothers with social problems. The book's publication in 1962 placed it at a watershed moment for British social science as the gentlemanly style developed by self-taught figures such as Titmuss gave way to a more professionalised and less moralistic approach which re-shaped academic practice. 1962 was also the year in which Oakley commenced her undergraduate studies, which exposed her to both ways of practising social science, epitomised respectively in the two dons who taught her sociology, Bryan Wilson and A. H. (Chelly) Halsey. The latter had the greater effect on her and was more in tune with the newly-formed Social Science Research Council which was to fund her PhD as well as later research projects (some under its successor title the Economic and Social Research Council). The funding body recognised Oakley's housework study as among the top 50 projects that it had supported in the 50 years from 1965, notwithstanding her several criticisms of the principles underpinning its funding mechanisms. Further recognition of her work, along with criticism, has been forthcoming from a range of sources, and for a variety of elements in a career that she has described as involving a shift from sociologist to social scientist. All the while she has retained her original convictions regarding the purpose of academic and related endeavours and their potential to contribute to changing the world for the better through moving towards a less gender-divided society.

Oakley's life follows a trajectory in which breaking new ground is interwoven with frequent revisiting of familiar themes. Family relationships exercise a particular magnetism, repeatedly pulling her to consider the part played in who we become by people closest to us. Her relationship to her parents figures prominently in this respect, including not only what she has written directly on the subject but also through her engagement with the intellectual legacy that her father bequeathed. The peace movement provides another recurrent theme. It provided a route into political activism for the youthful Oakley, whose parents' long-held anti-war sentiment had been reinforced by the practical challenges which their daughter's wartime birth presented.

Oakley's biography of Baroness Wootton included a description of her role in the formation of the Campaign for Nuclear Disarmament that Oakley had joined as a teenager. Wootton had been widowed four decades previously during the First World War. Women's pacifism and their campaigns against war at that time were given equal prominence with welfare in the title of Oakley's book on first wave feminists, though an earlier biographical account of Millicent Fawcett had recognised that some prominent feminists had supported the war, and nationalism and militarism more generally. Although she noted in various places in her work that warfare could unintentionally bring useful scientific and technical advances, Oakley was persuaded by arguments that excessive expenditure on armaments comes at the cost of people's health, a sentiment shared by some of the children that she and Gillian Bendelow studied. Her methodological insights on interviewing were taken into account in Sasha Roseneil's sociological study of the women's peace camp at Greenham Common whose members opposed the siting of nuclear weapons there in the 1980s and were much demonised for doing so (although Oakley applauded their bravery). Such episodes of contested representation relate to another recurrent theme, that of the politics of truth. Oakley's work grapples with fact and fantasy and their interplay, or with scientific endeavour and poetic licence. Her novels include among their *dramatis personae* sociologists and their research participants, along with quotations from de Beauvoir, while her academic publications highlight the openness to different interpretations that characterise terms like 'women confined' and 'mean values' and questions such as 'who cares?' Imagination plays a key role in both literary expression and scientific endeavour and complicates efforts to determine what is real about the world and the men, women, children and other creatures that inhabit it. An important lesson flowing from this is that alternative visions are available and deserve serious consideration.

2

ANN OAKLEY'S LIFE AND CAREER

Extensive information exists in the public domain about Ann Oakley's life and career, much of which she has put there herself. Autobiographical elements pervade her writings, sometimes indirectly (such as when characters in her novels follow paths which resemble those which she has trodden). Accounts of lives are always selective, as Oakley remarked in relation to the gaps in Barbara Wootton's autobiography about which readers can only speculate. Her biography of the Baroness did shed light on things that her subject had not mentioned, including matters that she suspected Wootton may have preferred to stay hidden. Telling the story of a life necessarily involves ethical decisions about what to disclose, and Oakley's biographical accounts of her parents illustrate how delicate such decisions can be when the narrator has had access to the private lives of their subjects, encompassing the realm of family secrets. Her father's saint-like public reputation and its associated legends, myths and fables did not always square with her knowledge of his routine home life. During his weekly telephone conversations with his widowed mother, for example, his attention would surreptitiously (and in Oakley's view forgivably) be diverted to reading papers or writing letters. Family relationships provide rich sources of insight into human foibles, and close observation of her father helped Oakley to understand that a person who does not express emotions may nevertheless feel anger, irritation, hatred or resentment or (more positively) love, affection, camaraderie and joy. Her mother was less restrained than her father in showing her emotions, and from this, Oakley learnt that women sometimes engage in competition with each other for men's favour but can also be more open and honest. Long after her parents' deaths, she has continued to reflect on questions about identity that were rooted in her upbringing and her formative experience of personhood for which they were responsible.

Ann Rosamund Titmuss was born in a London hospital on 17th January 1944, in the penultimate year of the Second World War when the city was still subject to aerial bombardment. Had the birth not been premature, her mother would have been 41 when Ann was delivered; her father was 36, and she was their only child. The Titmusses married in 1937 and took a scholarly as well as a personal interest in reproduction, including jointly writing a book about the declining birth rate, a trend that they regarded as antithetical to social progress. Before their marriage, her mother, Kathleen (Kay) Miller, who came from a middle-class background, had been engaged in social work with unemployed people. This provided a point of connection to her father Richard's interests in demography and poverty that grew out of his early career in the field of insurance. These interests led her father to join the Eugenics Society in 1937, identifying with its more progressive elements that were compatible with his political views about the influence of social conditions rather than its more reactionary, biologically deterministic wing for which it is better known. He was at this time also a Liberal Party member, and not alone in combining Liberal Party and Eugenics Society affiliations; another figure who did so was William Beveridge, whose 1942 Report on social insurance constituted the foundation stone of the modern welfare state.

Titmuss's activism facilitated access to prominent academic and political circles. He was appointed Professor of Social Administration at the LSE at the age of 43, despite being largely self-taught; he had left formal education at 14 and did not possess a degree. One version of Oakley's father's story, promulgated by his wife, is that of the self-made man, but his childhood was not particularly deprived, and the social networks that he cultivated provided opportunities for advancement. It is also clear that Kay Titmuss made considerable contributions to her husband's success, like many women of her generation forgoing prospects for her own career advancement to support a spouse's upward mobility.

Oakley's parents gave off mixed messages about what was expected of her and about the person she might become. The Titmusses' parenting styles reflected their different social class backgrounds but nevertheless embodied the prevailing ideas of the time about what would become Oakley's core concern, the contrasting standards and patterns of behaviour according to which men and women (and, by extension, boys and girls) are expected to live. Efforts while she was growing up to make sense of her parents' relationship and of family relationships more generally meant that she was already puzzling over gender relations, long before her pioneering analyses were committed to print. Her father's death aged 65 came soon after the publication of her first book, *Sex, Gender and Society*, to which he responded coolly (to her understandable disappointment). Father and daughter were not able to reconcile their divergent opinions about the arguments that she was advancing through her academic work. Her mother outlived her father by 14 years, but also seemed reluctant to approve her daughter's trajectory of advocating feminist causes and successfully combining motherhood and a career. After the achievements of first wave feminism in securing greater recognition for women in the United Kingdom (including in 1928 rights to vote equal to those of men), the pace of change towards gender equality had slackened. For Oakley's mother's generation, men's careers took priority over women's, and the principal roles of wives were reproduction and the efficient running of the domestic sphere. Oakley rejected a future for herself as a dutiful daughter and wife. Encouraged by her parents' commitment to education and to independent-mindedness more generally, she refused the forced choice between marriage and career with which women of her mother's generation had been confronted. Books such as Betty Friedan's *The Feminine Mystique* could also be found in her parents' home, indicating that they were not altogether closed off to radical thinking about women's place in the world.

Greater clarity about Oakley's childhood was achieved in adulthood through revisiting her family of origin with the aid of new information and by adopting a historically informed comparative perspective. Oakley was 43 when her mother died, and one of the things she bequeathed was a suitcase containing assorted items which had been carefully assembled to provide insights into her background. There was sufficient material on which to base a book about her parents' lives together. Its title, *Man and Wife*, conveys how marriage at that time was conceived and normalised based on supposedly complementary roles that in practice worked to men's advantage. The phrase used to conclude the conventional marriage ceremony cannot be inverted: 'woman and husband' makes no sense. Women are positioned through their relationship to men, as wives, but not vice versa. Women were, in Simone de Beauvoir's words, *The Second Sex*. An instructive revelation in *Man and Wife* is that Oakley's parents were sufficiently confident of having a son that they had settled on the name Adrian and purchased gender-appropriate blue wool to knit baby clothes. Learning that she was originally spoken of as a boy implied gendered expectations and suggested a reason for the disappointment that she sensed they felt in their child. A predictable desire followed to exceed the limited ambitions mapped out for her. It is telling that Oakley's mother was unfulfilled by the housewife role, describing herself as a 'discontented dishwasher', and that sketches of her parents by a teenage Ann show her father at a desk and her mother at a sink. Later, in *Father and Daughter*, Oakley expanded on how her parents had influenced her life. The book's genesis lay in the unveiling of an English Heritage blue plaque, as a public acknowledgement of her father's achievements, on the house in Acton where she had grown up. All parents subject children to pressures to behave well, but having a father with an entry in *Who's Who* and later honoured with a CBE (and a mother intensely proud of such recognition) quite possibly intensified the reception of injunctions to be good.

The private girls' school Haberdashers' Aske's which Ann attended emphasised service and obedience. Her move to this school at the age of 6 was followed soon after by the family's relocation from a cramped flat in Chiswick to the house on which the blue plaque honouring her father would later be erected. Her formal education had begun aged 4 at Oxford College, a small local private establishment about which she had fuzzy memories of achievement despite fear of failure, in a building later to become a women's refuge. Her schooldays were not fondly remembered; although she performed well academically, she made few friends and the school assessed her prospects more narrowly than she did. Her experiences provided an early lesson that adherence to what other people identify as codes of good behaviour may, paradoxically, leave one feeling bad, and cumulatively result in a sense of being an impersonator, a misfit, an intruder, a marginal figure, an outsider, a stranger or even an alien. Oakley left the institution at the earliest opportunity, aged 16. Outside of school, Oakley's home life was ordered and more austere than her father's professorial salary might have been expected to allow, in part because that income was also used to support her paternal grandmother across decades of widowhood. Oakley's grandmothers were distant figures uninterested in the emotional connection to grandchildren that has come to characterise the current generation, and wider networks of relatives reinforced the notion of family as a realm of conformity and obligation rather than encouragement to fulfil individual potential. More stimulating to the young Oakley were the numerous prominent figures that she met through her parents, people who shared her father's mission to reshape thinking about social policy. Visitors to the house in Acton included Barbara Wootton (whose biography she would later write), Richard Tawney (the writer on equality who would figure in another of her archive-based investigations) and Pearl Jephcott (about whose inspirational embodiment of the imagination and determination required by female sociological researchers to make a career in a male-dominated university environment Oakley would also write).

Chiswick Polytechnic, where Oakley studied for her 'A' levels, released her from uniform wearing and was an altogether freer learning environment than her school. Encouragement to make up her own mind about the merits of Jane Austen and other literary classics stimulated cultural inquisitiveness and greater self-expression, including political expression. She joined organisations opposed to capital punishment (not outlawed for murder in the United Kingdom until 1965) and to nuclear weapons (which remains an ongoing campaign). She also found it liberating to have escaped single-sex education, although she was to re-acquaint herself with female-only institutions during her undergraduate years based at Somerville College, Oxford. Encouraged by her father and aided by his LSE colleague Brian Abel-Smith, she had sat the Oxford University entrance examinations. Admitted on the strength of one exceptional paper, she began her degree studies in Philosophy, Politics and Economics in the autumn of 1962. She was 18 and living outside of London for the first time, apart from the periods in the year that she was born that she spent with her mother as evacuees from the wartime bombing. With hindsight, she reflected that she might have felt more at home and received a more conducive education by attending one of the newly founded universities that started admitting students in the early 1960s such as the University of Sussex (which had, incidentally, sought unsuccessfully to appoint Charles Wright Mills to its staff). Oakley found Oxford's pedagogic approach arid and unrelated to the real world, or at least to the real world beyond the upper classes; she also objected to the gender-biased focus on economic man and to the double standards in university rules. It was Chelly Halsey, a friend of her father's, whose tutoring in sociology left the most enduring legacy from her studies, including introducing her to Mills's notion of the sociological imagination and the potential of expressing oneself through sociological poetry. Sociology was a new option in her final year and provided at least partial answers to questions that intrigued her such as how individuals are shaped by the social circumstances of their times and places.

Oxford also provided the context in which the 20-year-old Ann Titmuss (as she then was) met and married Robin Oakley, a slightly older social anthropology postgraduate student. The marriage needed the approval of her college and also of her parents because she was under 21. She was pleased to leave behind her parents' surname, having been teased about it at school. She was, however, less enamoured of being called 'Mrs Robin Oakley', as her father had done in the preface to one of his books in which her new husband also featured among those thanked for comments on earlier drafts. Robin Oakley's influence was greater on Titmuss's last and most celebrated book, *The Gift Relationship*, directing him to the anthropological literature on altruism which became central to his analysis of blood donation. By the time of the book's publication in 1970, however, a rift had developed between Titmuss and his daughter and son-in-law, and no acknowledgement to them appeared among those thanked in the preface. Following her wedding, Oakley completed her degree and wrote numerous things that went unpublished, including two novels; she had long had the ambition to be a writer, but the publishers prevaricated and ultimately turned them down. Having moved back to London (where Robin had become a lecturer at Bedford College), she also provided research assistance on various short-term projects, both academic (including at the Institute of Social Studies of Medical Care) and in market research. She found housework unfulfilling, and the birth of her first two children, a son and a daughter, before she was 24 brought on what was known in both popular culture and medical circles as post-natal depression. Contrary to this medicalised perspective, Oakley regarded her feelings of exhaustion and distress as understandable responses to unrelieved domestic responsibility, however much her children also prompted love and related emotions. One of her research projects exploring motherhood would later make clearer that she lacked social support and reassurance; at the time, feelings of personal failure to live up to what was expected of her weighed heavily.

Undertaking a research degree may not have seemed an ideal option for a hard-pressed mother of young children in her mid-20s, but this was what Oakley did. Her husband was lecturing and completing his PhD, and a book in his study about workers' alienation which said nothing about housework provided her with her topic. The idea that the sociology

of housework was an appropriate PhD subject met some
scepticism, and Oakley felt that George Brown, her supervisor
at Bedford College, never fully grasped her purpose in
studying housework as work not given proper recognition.
Despite these obstacles, 5 years on from its commencement in
1969, the study had led to not only a successful thesis
(defended at a marathon four-hour viva) but two books on the
subject, *The Sociology of Housework* and *Housewife*, while
the further book *Sex, Gender and Society* had been written
during the studentship-funded project. By the age of 30, she
had produced two children and several academic publications,
and she looked to continue defying convention by combining
motherhood and a career. Aware that the route into teaching
did not appeal, she applied to the Social Science Research
Council for funding to investigate the process of becoming a
mother. This provided the opportunity to continue satisfying
her curiosity by discovering unexpected things about other
people's lives. The project brought Oakley into direct contact
with the medical establishment, which was to become an
enduring focus of her research attention. Her own experiences
of having children had involved difficult encounters with
medical professionals, including the diagnosis of post-natal
depression as well as the processes directly related to giving
birth, and she knew from mothers interviewed for the
housework study that she was not alone in this. In addition,
Oakley's father had died pre-retirement in 1973 of lung cancer, erroneously diagnosed initially as a frozen shoulder. Over
the next few years, Oakley herself was diagnosed with cancer
of the tongue (which was treated successfully), and suffered
the pain and sadness of two miscarriages, one of which could
also have been life-threatening for her. She resisted a doctor's
suggestion of sterilisation made on the grounds that her son
and daughter constituted a complete family and went on to
have her third child (a second daughter) in 1977.

Oakley's difficult medical encounters illustrate the risk of feminist research directing attention uncomfortably close to home. Her feminism had been incipient in her undergraduate days, and took further time to become more fully fledged, assisted by her experience of marriage and motherhood. The language of being captive and wedlocked gained currency as women in her position sought to make sense of their predicament. Oakley found herself on a steep learning curve as she joined a local women's liberation group in 1971 and discovered the extent to which feelings that she had wrestled with in isolation resembled problems shared by others. This fitted what Mills had written in *The Sociological Imagination* about personal troubles also being public issues, and about private lives feeling like a series of traps. Consciousness-raising activities gave Oakley the confidence to reject the idea that medication offered a solution to her unhappiness with conventional feminine roles, to consider instead that depression was linked to oppression, and to look for ways out of these problems collectively through social and political change. The broader women's liberation movement reinforced the notion of the political character of personal matters by articulating demands that included state-provided childcare, reproductive rights and workplace equality. Oakley's feminist perspective was still taking shape when she wrote *Sex, Gender and Society*, and she later acknowledged the criticism made on theoretical grounds that the book paid insufficient attention to patriarchal structures of power. Feminist thinking evolved rapidly even in the short period between conducting her PhD fieldwork and the stage of writing up her findings. The women who in 1971 introduced her to the local women's liberation group had been far from representative of her interviewees; more typical responses to her interview question about women's liberation came from women who had few points of engagement with and little sympathy for the agenda of abolishing traditional gender roles embodied in family relationships which she advocated at the end of *Housewife*. Her participants may have disliked housework and longed for its burdensomeness to be eased, as Oakley had, but it did not follow that they were revolutionaries actively seeking the abolition of the housewife role.

Oakley's efforts to redress the entrenched lack of awareness of gender inequalities elicited not only anticipated criticism of bias from mainstream academic and journalistic reviewers but also more unexpected charges from fellow feminists for insufficient radicalism. Social movements typically contain a spectrum of standpoints, and Oakley sought to promote dialogue between others' feminist thinking and her own. Juliet Mitchell's psychoanalytical leanings contrasted with Oakley's sociological approach, but together they edited three broad-ranging books about feminism: *The Rights and Wrongs of Women* in 1976, *What is Feminism?* a decade later and *Who's Afraid of Feminism?* in 1997. These books engaged with the politics of the women's movement, including preparedness to ask difficult questions about the nature of solidarity between women (both past and present), about the challenge of defining feminism and about how to evaluate the effects of second wave feminism, including the backlash to which it gave rise. Oakley's experience of supportiveness from her women's liberation group in Ealing included them meeting her on her return from an early seminar that she had nervously accepted the invitation to give. The group's shared focus included practical activities like fund-raising for local projects as well as discussion of ideas like international revolution. This small group of about a dozen women found it liberating to forge a shared purpose in the face of common experiences of second-class status, but even here differences between them had to be negotiated, and at a reunion a decade later, one of them recalled this not always being done as kindly as it might have been. A particularly divisive issue both locally and in the wider movement concerned the desirability or otherwise of marriage to and living with men. Separatists argued for women to form communal households apart from men, and when some extended the excluded group to cover male children as well, Oakley saw this as taking the critique of the nuclear family too far from a personal as well as a political point of view. A further pressing question was whether feminists were engaged in promoting the interests of women or caring for humanity and planet Earth more broadly.

Just as her father's death had led Oakley to take stock of her life and achievements, so her mother's passing in 1987 prompted similar reflection, updating the assessment contained in her candid semi-autobiographical account *Taking It Like a Woman* which had been published when she was 40. Like other books of hers, it reached an international audience, partly through translation. In the 14 years of her mother's widowhood, Oakley had given birth to a third child following two miscarriages, overcome serious health issues, become more distant emotionally from her mother, and negotiated a legal separation from her husband, having previously sold her wedding ring and rejected its symbolism of ownership. Academically, she had consolidated her credentials through further research and writing and improved her job security via the position of Deputy Director of the Thomas Coram Research Unit. This appointment followed a succession of short-term posts including some based at Oxford working with the epidemiologist and health services researcher Iain Chalmers with whom she shared interests not only in the study of childbirth but also in research methodology and policy relevance. In the same way that her doctoral research became considerably broader than its initial specification, her study of the processes surrounding becoming a mother grew into something much larger, a wide-ranging critique of women's social control by medicine. *Becoming a Mother* (later re-published as *From Here to Maternity*) performed a similar function for childbirth as *The Sociology of Housework* had in portraying what being a housewife is like, namely to expose how actual experiences diverge from expectations. A second book from the project, *Women Confined*, explored how childbirth is managed and how women are controlled as they become mothers. Additional publications about medicine and motherhood arose out of further projects: *The Captured Womb* delved into the history of pregnant women's care, while *Social Support and Motherhood* brought additional research methods to bear on the substantive issue of social and medical influences on pregnancy outcomes and reflected on the nature of research findings and their potential to enhance the promotion of good health. Britain's apparent poor record of perinatal care meant that there was an urgent need to pay attention to innovative practical interventions, even if no consensus existed about how best to assess their results.

People's trajectories are frequently too multifaceted to allow simple periodisation, although one commentator did differentiate an 'old' Oakley from the supposedly 'new' one who had in the 1980s moved away from qualitative research to employ quantitative methods like randomised controlled trials. Oakley rebutted this mischaracterisation by pointing out that she had always been open to quantitative methods. Nevertheless, other developments around this time signalled important shifts taking place. Unhappy at being passed over as Director of the Thomas Coram Research Unit when Barbara Tizard retired, Oakley left in 1990 to found and direct the Social Science Research Unit (SSRU), with social policy as well as sociology in her accompanying professorial title. She rejected the view of policy-relevant researchers as complicit in the exercise of state control, arguing instead that social scientists had opportunities to make a difference to people's lives by influencing policymaking, including that of transnational bodies such as the World Health Organization (WHO). WHO work took her to countries such as China which had very different policy regimes. Her view was reinforced through studying the provision made for new mothers, and she identified possible improvements via publications that included a book co-written with the Danish midwife Susanne Houd, *Helpers in Childbirth*. Chalmers's work on systematic reviewing of research evidence proved highly influential in the development of Oakley's thinking about the evaluation of policy provision at a time of extensive public debate regarding women's position more generally. Campaigners' need for reliable evidence was heightened by concerns that the effects of feminist-inspired initiatives to better women's lot were being halted or reversed by Thatcherite policies of welfare state retrenchment brought in during the 1980s under the UK's first female Prime Minister. Two further shifts in Oakley's life in her forties involved the resumption of cycling as a preferred mode of transport and creative writing. Poetry was included among her collected essays, and she resumed writing novels, this time finding publishers. The positive reception of *The Men's Room* (the title of which referenced Marilyn French's *The Women's Room*) saw it reworked as a television series, and the book's publication in 1988 was followed by six further novels (including one under a pseudonym, Rosamund Clay) in just over a decade. In one of these six, *Scenes Originating in the Garden of Eden*, the main character swops London for village life, which has similarities to Oakley's acquisition of a country cottage as a retreat where solitude away from the intensity of the capital facilitated creativity.

While writing novels can be a solitary activity, Oakley's SSRU work involved extensive collaboration with both social scientific researchers and users of their output. Her vision as Director of the SSRU was influenced by the benefits that systematic reviewing of evidence had brought to medical research through the analysis of the findings of projects that had been conducted with demonstrable quality. From relatively small beginnings, the activities of the SSRU grew rapidly, not least through the establishment of the Evidence for Policy and Practice Information and Co-ordinating Centre (the EPPI Centre) which came to account for the majority of SSRU's staff of several dozen and which continues to thrive. Oakley's direct responsibility for SSRU activities lasted until her successor David Gough took over the reins. During the period 1990–2005, her pattern of publications shifted to being predominantly joint-authored reports, articles, books and chapters in a wide range of policy-related fields such as health education, always paying close attention to the methodological rigour of the underpinning research and the uses to which it might be put. A recurrent concern in this work related to the variability of how well the details of the procedures that researchers employ are reported, ranging from exhaustive to seriously lacking. Because of this problem, the process of synthesising research results was uneven, and Oakley's attention was drawn not only to the issue of careful research design and its implementation but also to more fundamental epistemological questions of knowledge claims. These she explored in various places, including in debates about the relative merits of quoting and counting where she argued against the idea that feminist research necessarily had greater affinity with qualitative methods. More broadly, she discouraged the prolongation of the paradigm wars that featured adversarial attachments to quantitative and qualitative methods. Her book *Experiments in Knowing* acknowledged the discrepancies routinely thrown up in scientific research (including her own), and she noted that these highlight the difficulties of sustaining any simple distinction between fact and fiction, or truth and invention, but she also set out the reasons why working as a social scientist and as a novelist constituted distinct activities.

Oakley's engagement with the policy-related dimensions of social science was given further impetus by becoming her father's literary executor after her mother died. *Man and Wife* (1996) reflected on Richard and Kay Titmuss's lives prior to his appointment as the LSE's first Professor of Social Administration. The enduring significance of his critique of market-based approaches to welfare in *The Gift Relationship* provided the rationale a quarter of a century on from its original publication for Oakley and John Ashton to bring out an expanded and updated edition in 1997. Following this, Oakley and further collaborators brought out two collections of Titmuss's essays, also with new commentaries on the continuing relevance of his ideas, *Welfare and Wellbeing* (2001) and *Private Complaints and Public Health* (2004). Having long reflected on whether his career represented a role model for her, consideration of their two trajectories and the interconnections between them resulted in *Father and Daughter* (2014), combining biography and autobiography. Oakley judged that, had he not died prematurely, her father would have eschewed retirement in favour of continuing to work, just as she herself has done, driven to keep asking social scientific questions and seeking to answer them in ways that are intellectually rigorous and relevant practically. Her books have continued to range widely. *Gender on Planet Earth* (2002), for example, took as its focus global developments including pressing environmental concerns, and promulgated a moral passion akin to that which informed her father's critique of existing arrangements in publications such as *The Irresponsible Society*. Another wide-ranging book was *Fracture* (2007), which explored themes of embodiment, identity and the problem of ageing, weaving these around an autobiographical narrative of the consequences of an injury to her right arm. The experience also brought to mind a point made in her becoming a mother study that there can be considerable discrepancies between people's experiences of medical attention and the records kept by medical professionals. Four further books based on archival work tell the stories of the life and work of Barbara Wootton (*A Critical Woman*, 2011), of the trailblazing women of feminism's first wave (*Women, Peace and Welfare*, 2018), of the overlooked spouses of four eminent men whose eminence owed much to those wives' supportive endeavours (*Forgotten Wives*, 2021), and of the women who championed domestic science (*The Science of Housework*, 2024).

Long careers provide opportunities to re-visit issues first encountered many years earlier. Undertaking the re-study of the process of becoming a mother revealed much about changes and continuities in women's experiences since the 1970s and also proved instructive about research practice and about the reception of publications. Returning to participants 37 years later was revealing about memory and forgetfulness because, to Oakley's surprise, not all of them remembered being interviewed by her multiple times, nor in one case Oakley's presence at her child's birth. In addition, the publication arising from the original project which designated interviewing women as a contradiction in terms illustrated how arguments advanced may be used by other researchers in ways that are at odds with an author's intentions; Oakley disagreed with those who read it as supporting the case that feminist sociology prioritises the use of qualitative methods. Nor did she wish to stand by all aspects of her original argument, finding some parts of it naïve, just as similar shortcomings of her first books on gender and on housework were acknowledged when revisiting those in prefatory remarks written for their 1985 republication. Criticisms of perspectives appearing outdated are to be expected even more for work published several decades ago, but these concerns were outweighed for Oakley and her publishers by the case for bringing out new editions of *Sex, Gender and Society* (2015), and of *The Sociology of Housework, From Here To Maternity*, and *Social Support and Motherhood* (all 2019), respectively 43, 45, 40 and 27 years after they originally appeared. Previously *The Ann Oakley Reader* (2005) had assembled elements from three and a half decades of her work. In the Preface to that collection Oakley reflected on how some ideas that were once fresh and unusual become absorbed into mainstream thinking while others move from being new to seeming old-fashioned and on the path to redundancy as historical curiosities; a particularly interesting third group avoid that fate by appearing new for a second time. This fits the historical focus of much of Oakley's recent writing, both her archive-based books and her most recent (2022) novel, *The strange lockdown life of Alice Henry*.

Oakley's publication record is extensive, including well over 30 books, no fewer than 19 of them sole-authored academic works and a further eight novels, with co-authored books and jointly edited collections accounting for the rest. Journal articles, chapters in books, reports and other items take her total publications over 500, averaging 10 a year across her career. This remarkable record has been aided by drawing productively on personal experience. Her studies of housework and of becoming a mother made use of first-hand knowledge, and she could relate to family formation among women of her generation through her own marriage at the age of 20 (the average age of first time brides in England and Wales in 1964 was 22) and the subsequent dissolution of that marriage (an experience shared by nearly 30% of her cohort, and over 40% of some subsequent cohorts). She and her co-authors of *Miscarriage* (1984) estimated that at least 426,000 miscarriages occurred in Britain annually. Personal experiences of miscarriage among the three authors meant that they had figured in these statistics. Other women's experiences of medical matters will have resonated with Oakley's accounts of her episodes of ill-health from her childhood polio and insomnia onwards. A similar point about drawing on direct knowledge of her subject relates to her novels. In *The Men's Room*, Charity Walton is studying for a PhD in Sociology, and in *The Secret Lives of Eleanor Jenkinson*, the main character has two unpublished novels, while characters in the campus novel *Overheads* express the frustrations academics have regarding modern universities' byzantine financial accounting systems with which Oakley was all too familiar, it also having been a theme in *The Men's Room*. Furthermore, personal experience is central to Oakley's more autobiographical works. *Taking It Like a Woman* includes discussion of her miscarriages, and *Father and Daughter* relates a deep but sometimes difficult relationship. She disagrees that autobiographical writing is self-indulgent, treating it instead as an important vehicle for women seeking to challenge cultural misrepresentations. This is especially true if they have lived their lives at odds with prevailing social norms, as Oakley considered her heroine Barbara Wootton, her sociological hero Mills and herself to have done.

In the first novel that Oakley wrote shortly after completing her undergraduate degree (which remained unpublished), the main character expressed the youthful ambition to be the embodiment of her generation. Much later, Oakley reflected on the potential of the story of one life to illuminate broader patterns of social arrangements and social change, and how sociology and novels offer different means of doing this. Accounts need to be presented in ways that are relatable if audiences are to identify with the portrayal of an individual experience. Oakley's preparedness to experiment with various types of dissemination has assisted in reaching this goal. Her account in *Fracture* of losing the ability to hold a pen (which was central to her deep-seated identity as a writer) had as part of its purpose conveying something of the experience of disability. Loss of this bodily function was not on a par with the most profound disabilities, but her description nevertheless provided insights into the meaning of disabling conditions and social responses to them to which others could relate. There are, moreover, parallels between women's position as outsiders in a man's world and people with disabilities' exclusion from the world built around able-bodied norms. A different form of hierarchy found in the medical world concerns relations between experts and non-experts, and in *From Here to Maternity*, Oakley reversed normal publishing conventions by giving greater prominence to what the mothers interviewed for the project themselves had said, with a corresponding reduction in the status given to her own authorial expertise. Oakley had longstanding misgivings about medical expertise and its expression in the process of medicalisation that treated women patients as passive participants in proceedings. Over time, this developed into a broader critique of expert knowledge and of the knowledge claims made by a variety of groups beyond doctors, including psychoanalysts, sociobiologists and economists. Oakley has been able to attract the attention of a wide audience among people with shared doubts about experts whose elegant theories have difficulties with, and may run counter to, everyday experience.

Proficient researchers need what Oakley and others call a nose for identifying good questions to ask. Concerns about experts' remoteness from everyday experience led her to emphasise research questions having resonance with research participants (who, ideally, should also find subsequent publications accessible). Engaged participants can ask many things when interviewers give them the opportunity; no fewer than

878 questions arose during 178 interviews in the becoming a mother project, for example. Research questions also grapple with intellectual puzzles, even if at times a researcher is alone in thinking these worth pursuing. Oakley was in this isolated position when she decided her PhD would focus on housework and why women are considered so suited to doing it. This project quickly repaid her faith by leading to consideration of the connections between biological and social processes and between bodies and cultures. The concept of gender became central to her efforts to answer questions about domestic life and family ties, about motherhood and medicine, about social science and research knowledge and about feminism and the history of efforts to recalibrate relationships between women and men. These questions reflect interests that range from the broad scale, asking (for example) what feminism is and what it has achieved, to more specific issues, such as listing the parts of a body that one can do without or how people adjust to loss. Regarding this latter subject, Oakley found useful Peter Marris's ideas, including his metaphor of identity resembling a clothes horse on which various garments could be draped, thereby conveying desired impressions to onlookers. The point that appearances can be deceptive, that things are not always what they seem, has relevance in all manner of contexts, from the practice of cross-dressing (which, Oakley noted, 6% of Americans engage in, according to a 1993 publication) to official statistics' potential to mislead us about work, crime, household structure and much else. Childhood holidays with relatives had taught Oakley that apparently blissful marriages could turn out to be otherwise. As a sociologist, she was soon using such insights to explore the notion of happy families and the reasons why expectations and reality diverged.

3

GENDER, HOUSEWORK AND MOTHERHOOD

Ann Oakley's first publication was entitled 'The myth of motherhood'. It was a short piece in *New Society* that came out in February 1970, just months into her PhD research on housework. *New Society* was a weekly magazine aimed at a broad audience through contributions written in a pithy, accessible style. Despite its brevity, Oakley's article anticipated themes that she would subsequently expand upon. In particular, she drew on various sources to challenge the notion that the sex roles that gave primacy to motherhood in women's lives had biological foundations. The anthropological studies that she cited pointed instead to cultural influences on what tasks are allocated to women and men, and this perspective offered a better explanation of the significant variations found between societies and of shifting patterns in specific cases. Her doubts about the extent to which the male/female distinction rested on natural foundations paved the way for the reworked contrast between 'sex' and 'gender' that would soon be advanced in her first book. Furthermore, by questioning the idea that women who combined motherhood with paid work were putting their offspring's well-being at risk, she was taking issue with the widely held notion of maternal deprivation which the psychologist John Bowlby famously propounded in relation to children raised in institutional care. Bowlby's ideas had been repurposed by campaigners seeking to associate the rising numbers of mothers in paid work with social problems among children and adolescents. Oakley was already familiar with more positive views about the growing proportion of married women in the labour market through the investigation conducted by her father's colleague Pearl Jephcott (amongst other studies). Oakley's debut publication had a tentative but thought-provoking quality, exploring discrepancies between prevailing assumptions and research findings which ran counter to the common sense of the time. The article's accompanying statistics about trends in women's work (both paid employment and unpaid housework) reinforced the case for further investigation of the changing position of women and pointed to the need for serious reconsideration of commonly accepted myths, notably the notion that a woman's place was in the home.

Oakley did not need to undertake this rethinking of contemporary women's lives from scratch. Published in 1962, Jephcott's *Married Women Working* had already disputed the canard of children suffering through mothers taking paid employment by reporting that their wages brought material benefits to the whole family. Other studies such as Alva Myrdal and Viola Klein's *Women's Two Roles* noted further advantages of married women undertaking paid work; among other things, it offered opportunities to broaden their social contacts and to escape the boredom of full-time domesticity. Combining these findings with additional data about growing support among husbands for wives having paid jobs encouraged some commentators speculate that relations between spouses were becoming less unequal and more symmetrical, even if the pace of change was slow; in the 1960s, only a minority of married women in the United Kingdom were employed, with much of that work part-time. A less sanguine interpretation was that women continued to be defined first and foremost not as paid workers (and certainly not as people with careers to build) but as housewives and mothers (either actually or prospectively). Conventional notions of femininity were nevertheless being challenged, for example, when Betty Friedan asked awkward questions about the idea that American women could achieve personal fulfilment primarily through marriage, motherhood and domesticity. In the United Kingdom, Hannah Gavron's 1966 book *The Captive Wife* reported on the sociological study of 96 married women in London who were under 32 years old and had at least one child under 5. These participants were recruited equally from among middle-class and working-class women, and a third of the mothers were in paid employment, with the proportion slightly higher among the former group. The much-vaunted emancipation of women sat uneasily alongside Gavron's findings that the roles of mother and worker were in tension and that motherhood was associated with being socially isolated and housebound. Landmark legal and political changes such as equal voting rights had not automatically ushered in a wider transformation in women's everyday lives. In addition, geographical mobility carried increased risk of loneliness for young mothers who no longer lived near to the kin networks that had provided close support in traditional working-class communities.

Oakley never discussed Gavron's work with her but knew her younger sister from university and had worked as a researcher for their academic father T. R. (Tosco) Fyvel shortly after leaving Oxford. Gavron had been born eight years before Oakley, providing a role model for her in several respects: both had artistic leanings and both successfully undertook PhDs at Bedford College in their twenties. Despite the college's pioneering role in promoting women's higher education, both had to assert themselves to study their chosen research topic in the face of scepticism in a male-dominated academic environment where doubts were expressed about the more qualitatively oriented approaches needed to capture the subjective dimensions of women's experiences. Both undertook investigations of topics in which a personal interest had developed through becoming wives and mothers by their early twenties, and both aimed to reach audiences beyond the academy by writing articles for publications such as *New Society*, as well as publishing book versions of their theses (in Gavron's case posthumously). Oakley's fieldwork focus on women's attitudes to housework explored the subject in greater depth than Gavron had been able to treat her broader coverage of housing, marriage, childcare, domestic organisation, social contacts, leisure and paid work, although Gavron's remark that many women spent 80 or more hours a week on housework showed alertness to its propensity to dominate women's lives. The decade of the 1960s separated their periods of fieldwork, during which time researchers who adopted a more self-consciously feminist approach began to emerge. Oakley was among these pioneers, but sympathetic to the predicament of predecessors like Gavron who had operated within the parameters of sexist frameworks that (for example) equated childcare with mothering, a set of tasks with which fathers at best 'helped', but for which they were not thought to have responsibility. Oakley had not attended the UK's first National Women's Liberation Conference in 1970, but she recalled attending the 1972 event, and involvement in the women's movement more generally, as inspirational encounters that opened up escape routes from lives experienced as captivity or imprisonment. Such interactions brought home that liberation required the radical reorientation of thinking and acting.

The research design of Oakley's PhD pre-dated her involvement with her local women's liberation group and was comparatively conventional. Several of the elements followed

Gavron's study, thus allowing some comparison of findings. Like Gavron, Oakley recruited equal numbers of working-class and middle-class women to facilitate discussion of how relevant material circumstances were to the experience of being a house-wife, although she stopped interviewing once she had reached a total of 20 in each group; she also expressed unease about allocating women to social classes based on their husbands' occupations. Her eligibility criteria for inclusion in the study resembled Gavron's in that the women had to be married, aged between 20 and 30 and had to have at least one child aged under 5. She decided in addition to focus on women born in Britain or Ireland in order to secure a homogeneous sample. Only six of Oakley's participants undertook paid work, thus making a higher proportion of her sample full-time housewives than those interviewed by Gavron. Oakley also followed Gavron by including the interview schedule as appendix II in *The Sociology of Housework*, concerned that readers of research reports should be provided with sufficient information about how the research was undertaken to judge it properly. Her thesis supervisor, George Brown, had joined Bedford College the year prior to Oakley's registration as a PhD student in 1969, and his influence can be detected in the inclusion of psycho-social questions about attitudes, satisfaction and identity. Following piloting, the interviewing process took place during the first three months of 1971. Recruitment of participants proceeded more smoothly than Gavron's, even though they both used General Practitioner patient lists (in different parts of London) to secure a sample; some of Oakley's prospective interviewees proved uncon-tactable, but no one contacted declined to be interviewed. The interview schedule contained over 100 questions, and the inter-views took on average two hours to complete. Interviewees' preparedness to talk to Oakley confounded the expectations of sceptics that they would have little to say about housework, and she acquired plentiful material to analyse, providing (as it turned out) the basis for two books, in addition to her thesis.

When *The Sociology of Housework* was published in 1974, Oakley already felt that things had changed significantly since she had conducted the fieldwork on which it was based, not least because women's liberation had greater prominence in the news and public debate as well as in her own life. New introductions to the book published in 1985 and 2019 saw Oakley remark that neither she nor anyone else would now approach the subject in the same way as she had originally, but even if some elements of the study (including the very word 'housewife') came to feel outdated, other aspects had more enduring significance, as its repeated republication attests. Oakley's study confirmed Gavron's comment about the long hours spent on housework: nearly half of her participants devoted 80 or more hours a week to it. The workload for all interviewees averaged 11 hours a day, a figure in line with findings from several studies conducted using different methodologies in urban settings in Britain and beyond (reported figures for rural settings being somewhat lower). Furthermore, the potential for easing this burden through improvements in domestic technology was not being realised in practice because the arrival of more efficient appliances came with pressure to raise standards, thereby confirming Friedan's axiom that housework expands to fill the time available. Oakley's argument was not, however, one of housewives' enslavement to machines; she emphasised instead their subordination to the ideology of feminine domesticity. The book conveyed compelling descriptions of the domestic routines around which housewives' lives were structured and which gave rise to dissatisfaction because of their monotony, socially isolated character, under-recognition and undervaluation, but the key question for Oakley was why women submitted themselves to such lives. Matters of identity figured prominently in her explanation. When asked to describe themselves, 'housewife' loomed large in their lexicon, along with family roles such as mother. Oakley regarded such self-images as the product of traditional domesticity being actively promoted as an expression of femininity, with each new generation of girls having instilled into them the aspiration to become home-making wives and mothers.

Oakley's findings supported her first article's argument that women's identity is wrapped up in ideals of motherhood. Not content to leave the matter there, however, in the book she sought to do much else besides questioning the myths surrounding the cultural construction of a good mother. Her principal ambition when commencing her thesis had been to develop the case that housework should be recognised as a form of work with many of the characteristics of paid work such as its centrality to people's identity and its potential for generating dissatisfaction and alienation, especially around those tasks which are dirty, repetitive, uncreative and/or unappreciated. Of course, the fact that much housework is performed in isolation stands as a contrast to paid work more typically being undertaken alongside other employees, as does the fact of housework generally being unpaid. Lack of remuneration figures prominently in reproducing housework's denigration as a lower status activity which is conveyed in the everyday expressions 'just housework' and 'just a housewife'. The widespread dissatisfaction with many aspects of the housewife role that Oakley uncovered only rarely translated into identification with the women's liberation movement and the alternatives to conventional families with which it was associated. She acknowledged that it was one thing for her and her fellow feminists to identify housewives as an oppressed group with the potential to be revolutionaries forging radically new ways of living, but quite another to develop strategies that could achieve such change. However much the language of sisterhood and solidarity was used to frame it, consciousness raising among housewives would be hampered if messages were perceived to be coming from supposedly enlightened middle-class women talking down to their working-class counterparts. Participating in small, women-only groups of the type that Oakley had herself found empowering held promise, particularly if discussions focused on everyday concerns rather than overly abstract theoretical discussions. That said, the theoretical puzzle remained of why women acquiesced to their subordination by internalising notions of womanhood constructed around problematic notions of domesticity and femininity, and here Oakley identified revered male sociologists as prominent culprits for the limited understanding of this issue or, more accurately, its misunderstanding.

Encouraged by her publisher, Oakley opened *The Sociology of Housework* with a critique of sociologists' portrayal of women. She argued that women were largely invisible within a discipline where the default position was to focus on men. Sociologists studied men at work, in politics, in education, in religion, in patterns of stratification, and in criminal and deviant activity. Oakley felt that this situation persisted because when Barbara Wootton had pointed out that researchers' neglect of women offenders produced distorted portrayals of criminality this had gone largely unheeded, as had related observations. Only in the sociology of the family (as it was then called, the definite article indicating the assumed pre-eminence of the nuclear family of a married heterosexual couple and their dependent children) did women occupy centre stage, and here invisibility was replaced by hackneyed stereotypes of domesticity. Oakley described women as over-visible in standard accounts of family life, referring both to the marginal presence of fathers in these accounts and to the treatment of women's domesticity as the cornerstone of their identity. She regarded this as a male-oriented perspective which was grounded not in women's actual experiences but in theorisation by male thinkers such as the American functionalist Talcott Parsons whose analysis highlighted the roles into which people were socialised. For Parsons, modern societies needed people to specialise by undertaking different but complementary roles, to everyone's benefit. Oakley raised two key objections to the application of these ideas to contemporary families. The first challenged the treatment of the roles of homemaker and breadwinner as equivalent, which in turn questioned the idea of marriage as a union of equals. The second objection was to women's portrayal as better suited to the homemaker role while the role of breadwinner went to men. To Oakley, explanations of such arrangements by reference to men's instrumental orientation and women's capacity to be expressive rested on unwarranted assumptions about biological differences between the sexes. These attributed to women a greater facility with emotions that come to the fore in home life while men were treated as more rational and better suited to the calculating culture found in paid work and elsewhere in the public realm.

Oakley saw this as blatantly sexist. Prevailing accounts of family relationships propagated the myth of female passivity, restricting women to the private sphere while families' active representation in the public sphere was undertaken by men. Parsons was, moreover, merely the latest in a long line of male sociologists whose portrayal of women reproduced unfavourable stereotypes. Sociology's so-called founding fathers were criticised for their views of women either as they were expressed in their writings or in their own domestic arrangements, and in some cases both. Oakley was unrepentant about criticising how figures such as Auguste Comte, Karl Marx and Émile Durkheim had treated their wives because she regarded their home lives as a relevant influence on what they wrote about women's position. Charles Wright Mills had made a similar point about American criminologists inheriting a parochial outlook from their small town backgrounds. And if sociologists' positions in society have a bearing on the analyses of social arrangements that they develop, then it is only a short step to ask whether a discipline that started out and continued to be male-dominated might operate with biases towards male-oriented perspectives in its accounts. The key point that things can be viewed from different angles, that (as Oakley put it) a way of seeing is also a way of not seeing, was one to which she would return repeatedly over her career. A female-oriented perspective would not necessarily be unbiased, but it did at least offer an antidote to the problem of women's invisibility in most fields of sociology and a corrective to their over-visibility in sociological accounts of family and domestic relations. The analysis of housework as work contributed to tackling both problems, and through this book and other publications, Oakley promoted the development of women's studies as a legitimate field of academic endeavour. She nevertheless kept faith with sociology's potential to fulfil its promise as a way of demystifying the world and later argued that sociology was at its best when practised by women and others in marginal positions because such vantage points gave them greater insight into social processes.

The companion volume to *The Sociology of Housework* which also arose from Oakley's PhD, *Housewife*, came out slightly earlier in 1974. It also demonstrated what is achievable by giving voice to women. The book's longest chapter is devoted to the stories of their lives as housewives as told to Oakley by 4 of the 40 interviewees. Oakley argued that the richness of these interview transcripts confirmed the value of careful listening, not least because these extended accounts provided a fuller and subtler picture than was provided by interviewees' initial answers to questions about whether they enjoyed housework. Apparent contradictions had to be scrutinised to reveal the ambivalence of their feelings about housework and the complexity of their perspectives on combining motherhood and paid work. Furthermore, by paying attention to detail, it became clear how important these women's mothers were as points of reference, sometimes as role models but in other cases as people whose trajectories should not be repeated. This point reinforced themes about social change that comprised most of the book. These set out how the housewife role had emerged historically alongside the process of industrialisation and was continually re-cast. Women's position in pre-industrial Britain gave them an independent status as productive workers rather than defining them in relation to others through their family relationships as mothers and dependent wives. Although industrialisation disrupted such arrangements, Oakley disputed the idea that industrial society operated with one pattern of gender roles and argued instead that three broad phases could be identified, each with distinctive features. In the first of these, from 1750 to 1841, the seeds of women's domesticity were sown as production was relocated to factories and families stopped working together. In the second phase, from 1841 to 1914, the decline of married women's employment outside of the home was reinforced by the Victorian ideology of female domesticity as something to which women were naturally suited. The third phase from 1914 to 1950 saw dependence on men and domestic ideology remain marked despite women achieving the right to vote and other legal entitlements, and notwithstanding their dramatically expanded involvement in paid work during the two world wars.

Oakley noted that the numbers of married women in paid work had risen steadily in the quarter century since 1950, but she regarded this as insufficient to dislodge the ideology of women's domesticity. Her parents had commented on a draft of the book despite her father's terminal illness, and she cited her father's finding that women accounted for five-sixths of the growth of the labour force of Great Britain in the 1950s, although caution was needed when interpreting such data. To begin with, much of this work was part-time, and thus more readily compatible with women continuing to hold responsibility for domestic life while men retained the breadwinner role. Secondly, women employees remained concentrated in a few sectors traditionally associated with domesticity such as nursing, teaching, retail and secretarial work, leaving other fields effectively as male preserves. Moreover, Oakley highlighted that marriage and parenthood have markedly different effects on women's and men's progression within employing organisations, particularly in the professions where she argued that the notion of a career was not gender neutral. Career-building required a masculine dedication to prioritising paid work duties that ran counter to women's actual or prospective domestic responsibilities. Such attitudes were reinforced by the growing influence of expert opinion regarding family welfare which extended the range of mothers' responsibilities for children's well-being. The achievement of women's equality to men also faced legal obstacles. Showing an aptitude for spotting what apparently trivial details might reveal, Oakley introduced her readers at the start of the book's opening chapter to the case of Albert Mills of Coventry who in 1970 sought to be treated as a housewife in relation to the 1965 National Insurance Act on the grounds that his wife Vera earned the household income while he had for 5 years kept house. The state ruled that Albert was ineligible for the dependent wife's benefit that Vera could have claimed had they conformed to the social norm with him the breadwinner and her the housewife. It was, according to the Department of Health and Social Security's lawyer, natural for housewives to be women; by implication it was unnatural for men to be.

The Mills case was reported in a national newspaper. Oakley noted that 1971 also saw a London newspaper cover the case of Terry Floyd and Carole Lloyd who had married knowing that in the eyes of the state they were both biologically female. Despite Floyd's self-identification as a man, they fell foul of the law prohibiting biological females becoming husbands. Oakley was interested in what such cases disclosed about the types of people that women and men can be. In principle, industrial society was opening up the possibility of males and females becoming equal, but cultural conceptions of masculinity and femininity stood as barriers to women's emancipation. Marriage represented a particularly powerful expression of patriarchal inequality, captured in the expression 'man and wife' that Oakley later used when writing about her parents' lives together. Oakley wanted something different for herself and her generation, notwithstanding that in her preface to *Housewife* she thanked her own family for giving her first-hand experience of being oppressed as a housewife. There is the germ here of a theme that decades later Oakley would develop in the book *Forgotten Wives* which elaborated on the myriad forms of support from their spouses that famous men had enjoyed; freedom from domestic responsibilities allowed them to concentrate on their work in the public sphere. In *Housewife*, Oakley outlined a way forward to a different future that involved nothing less than abolishing three things: the role of housewife, the family and gender roles. The first of these was necessary, she argued, because without it women would continue to be treated as lesser beings than men, even if the campaign of the time for wages to be paid for housework were successful. The second followed from the first, because families are a vital site for reproducing the association of women with domesticity, and the learning of gender roles more broadly. The third element of the political programme with which Oakley concluded her book was more ambitious still, but necessary because of the deep-seated character of gender role ideology and its associated stereotypes of human nature into which people have been moulded and to which they become inured.

Housewife and *The Sociology of Housework* both benefitted from the ideas contained in *Sex, Gender and Society*, Oakley's first book that was published in 1972. She wrote it having become frustrated with the muddled thinking around the competing explanations of sex roles framed in terms of biology and culture. She needed clarity about these issues to develop her analysis of housework, domesticity and femininity. Wider audiences also stood to benefit from a revitalised approach to these longstanding debates about the relative importance of nature and nurture as influences on people's development. She set about clarifying the distinction between people's biologically given elements and those that are culturally based (or, as some people express it, socially constructed). The term gender had already been coined but at that point had only limited circulation, principally among psychiatrists and psychoanalysts (who used it in a rather specialised sense); Germaine Greer and Kate Millett used the term differently but in a relatively undeveloped way. Oakley took the conundrum with which these authors were grappling, relating to the problematic equation of the male sex with masculinity and the female sex with femininity. She cut through their detailed considerations of abnormal sexuality by advancing a simple, bold proposition: that sex be the term used for what is biologically determined, and gender used for what is culturally determined. The book was commissioned by Paul Barker, the editor of *New Society* (to which Oakley had already contributed several articles) and was written in that magazine's style. Several photographs conveyed the diversity of women's activities in a range of contexts, from load carrying in Kenya to road mending in the Soviet Union. These reinforced her argument that the findings of anthropological and other research refute common-sense declarations about the work performed by women being biologically-determined. Written in only 6 weeks, the book had rough edges (for example, in terms of academic niceties around referencing), but it was carried along by its bravado in disputing the idea of women's natural predisposition to all things feminine. By adopting this stance, Oakley could construct her analysis of housework on clear conceptual foundations and justify her inclusion of historical and comparative material to properly contextualise her findings about the lives of housewives in west London in the early 1970s.

Sex, Gender and Society marks an important moment in the development of Oakley's thinking. Some aspects of it reflect the enduring influence of her undergraduate studies in philosophy, politics and economics. There is, for example, the scrupulous logic which she applied to the findings of biologists and medical scientists relating to the variability of human bodies, especially among those categorised as intersexuals whose particular combinations of genes and genitalia gave them an intermediate position between male and female. If a binary opposition between men and women cannot be sustained, it follows that sex constitutes more of a continuum than a dichotomy, thereby confounding the case that simple biological bases exist for men's masculinity and women's femininity. Political scientists' and economists' findings were also drawn upon to free women from biologically determined fates. Women's greater participation in politics could be expected to lead to less belligerent outcomes, including fewer wars, while freeing women from housework to participate in employment had potential to yield greater economic efficiency by making best use of their skills. The sociology encountered by Oakley at Oxford also featured in the book's critical discussions of the stereotypical roles into which people in industrial societies are socialised, but far greater prominence was given to the social anthropological literature to which Robin Oakley introduced her, which proved more thought-provoking.

Whereas sociologists could be guilty of offering justifications of the status quo, anthropologists captured the imagination with unsettling accounts of myriad ways in which relations between women and men could differ. Such anthropological reports highlighted the enormous variability of gender, rooted in cultural processes. This was also the lesson drawn from the historical material with which the book opened. Just as anthropologists make familiar social arrangements seem strange, historians' accounts of times past force us to rethink our preconceptions. Oakley's account drew particular attention to the ideas of earlier generations of feminists who challenged the common sense of their day. Gavron's likening of homes to prisons for wives had parallels in the early nineteenth century, not long after Mary Wollstonecraft's strictures in *A Vindication of the Rights of Woman* had challenged male authors' assertions of women's natural weakness and submissiveness.

Given their breadth, it is unsurprising that Oakley kept returning to the themes of *Sex, Gender and Society*. Woll-stonecraft provided a reference point for the title and content of her 1976 edited collection with Juliet Mitchell, *The Rights and Wrongs of Women*, alongside *The Wrongs of Women*, Charlotte Tonna's lesser known publication from the early Victorian period. As Oakley noted in *Housewife*, women could be found on both sides of the argument about whether female employment went against nature. In *Housewife*, Oakley extended her earlier discussion of women's treatment as subordinate to men to provide a more nuanced analysis of the process of inferiorisation; a woman may identify with the housewife role and with the status that accrues to her indirectly through her husband's employment and other positions in the public sphere. *Subject Women* noted that socialisation in families and in schools steered girls' aspirations in this direction, preparing them for a particular type of womanhood shaped more by marriage and motherhood than by careers and involving an emphasis on their bodily difference. The theme of bodily differences would be revisited by Oakley in *Fracture*, her autobiographical account of bodily misadventure. Another important aim of *Sex, Gender and Society* had been to acknowledge the power of myths, including the foundational myth of Adam and Eve which would resurface in Oakley's novel *Scenes Originating in the Garden of Eden* and in various research outputs. In a broader sense, Oakley's ambition for her first book's promotion of the concept of gender as part of re-thinking how biology and culture shape the forces constraining women's lives is present in everything that followed in her career (and in much feminist thinking more generally). The book's influence far exceeded Oakley's assessment of it as a modest contribution to debates, and while its timing was undoubtedly propitious, Oakley's ability to identify challenging research questions was also important. This knack also figured as her PhD endeavours concluded. Studying housework had revealed many things, but it was the critical importance for women's lives of becoming a mother, more than becoming a wife, that stood out as the next research priority.

The year 1974 saw Oakley awarded her PhD and *Housewife* and *The Sociology of Housework* published. She had already secured Social Science Research Council funding to study the transition to motherhood, focusing on social and medical aspects of first childbirth. This project, with interruptions for the birth of her third child in 1977 and for sick leave, was her principal academic focus for the rest of the decade. It built directly on the housework study, being, for example, motivated by a desire to investigate the subject realistically, stripped of romanticised misrepresentation. *Housewife* had moved directly from its chapter on myths of women's place that related to work (broadly defined) to the examination of myths of women's place that surrounded motherhood: they represented two sides of the same coin, the powerful notion that needed debunking of a woman's place being in the home. The transition to motherhood study was again designed to draw extensively on women's accounts, collected through interviews, to correct misperceptions and put the record straight. Like housework, motherhood was a topic about which Oakley could draw on personal experience, as well as on contemporary debates about how things could be improved, not least in relation to the much-misunderstood issue of post-natal depression. In other respects, the transition to motherhood project was considerably more ambitious. The aim of collecting data from interviewees at four points in time, two before birth and two after, meant that far more material would be generated, especially as the number of mothers with whom contact was sought was more than double. In the event, non-response and declining to participate reduced the number of prospective mothers interviewed to 66, and attrition for various reasons (which had been anticipated) meant that a further 11 did not complete all four interviews, but this still left Oakley with 220 transcripts from the 55 women whose participation continued. With each interview typically lasting over 2 hours, a total of 546 hours of material was collected from this part of the project. Even with the research assistance of Jenny Whyte (who conducted 55 of the 233 interviews), this was a huge undertaking.

The greater ambition of the transition to motherhood study was not only a matter of scale. Other methods besides interviewing were employed. Oakley attended births (including those involving six of the women in her interview sample) to witness women becoming mothers. In the London maternity hospital where the antenatal clinic that provided access to the sample of interviewees was based, she conducted other observations over several months. These included gathering material from parentcraft classes, baby clinics and consultations that women had with medical staff in either hospital wards or the outpatient antenatal clinic. Oakley took notes on 906 consultations between doctors and patients during 90 clinic sessions. In addition, she analysed her interviewees' hospital medical notes and surveyed the advice literature aimed at mothers. Most of the research's observational element was undertaken before the interviewing began in mid-1975, allowing the observations to inform the interview questions asked. Oakley's own experience of becoming a first-time mother had included rewards but also difficulties, including challenging episodes of surveillance, labelling and control by medical professionals, and this theme had also been mentioned in her housework study. The observations of other pregnant women's experiences of medicalisation confirmed the correctness of asking how typical her story was. This engagement with questions of medical practice relates in further ways to the project's ambition. The study involved requesting access to much more than a list of patients' contact details, and persuading a professor of obstetrics to allow such access succeeded only at the second attempt. There was, moreover, a much bigger literature about reproduction to address than there had been about the under-researched topic of housework. This literature was problematic in what it had to say about women and about the rationales offered for the medicalisation of childbirth, posing a different challenge to that of women's invisibility. It required engagement, and confrontation, with powerful medical and psychological paradigms as well as the sociological ones which had previously been the principal targets of her criticism. Sociologists were not let off the hook, as she characterised their treatment of family relationships as unimaginative (the opposite of Mills's sociological imagination), but she also had the ideological foundations of the psychological and medical science paradigm in her sights.

Speaking up about women's experiences of medical encounters involved challenging expertise and institutional reputations built up over decades, if not centuries. Fittingly, the first publications from the transition to motherhood project were historical essays about the management of childbirth: first a *New Society* piece, then Oakley's individual contribution to her co-edited collection *The Rights and Wrongs of Women*, the latter based on preliminary reading for the project rather than on fieldwork data. Oakley followed her previous practice of locating social arrangements in time and place. Just as housewives are products of industrial societies, a similar case can be made about the control exercised by predominantly male medical professionals leading teams that deploy increasingly complex technology in the delivery of babies. Oakley identified this male takeover of childbirth as a long-term shift from previous arrangements (still found in non-industrialised societies) in which midwives and other female practitioners brought different knowledge and practices to bear. The development of professionalised medical education and training and the trend towards births being hospital-based had the effect of marginalising women whose lay knowledge had been drawn upon when childbirth typically took place at home without the assistance of complicated technical monitoring and interventions. Oakley argued that in a long history of contestation over the process of reproductive care and who controls it, the case for medicalisation that was made in terms of bringing down mortality rates for babies and mothers deserved scrutiny because the statistics told a more complicated story than simple, linear progress. In addition, mortality rates were far from being the only consideration when looking at women's gains and losses from the triumph of medicalisation. The myth of female passivity which informed conceptions of femininity also figured in the way that medical professionals perceived their patients and reinforced the practices which took control of childbirth away from mothers. In the process, mothers' feelings became marginalised. Put another way, the ability to exercise control over childbirth was a long-standing issue, and campaigns of contemporary feminists regarding women's reproductive rights were part of this history of contesting the discrimination that women experienced and the misogyny in the ideologies that underpinned it.

Oakley's extensive preliminary reading did not prepare her for the shock of her first observation of a birth, a Caesarean section which she suspected the consultant invited her to attend to assess her resilience as a researcher. Passing this test secured Oakley access to medical professional culture. Spending time with medical professionals provided insights into a worldview that contrasted sharply with that articulated in interviews by first-time mothers. These mothers resembled those interviewed for the housework study in terms of their age (between 19 and 32 when they gave birth, with just over a half older than 25, the average age then for Britain). The study hospital was in a more affluent part of London, and this was reflected in the mothers being predominantly middle-class, whether measured by their partner's occupation or their own. Almost all interviewees were married; by the time of the fourth interview, only four cohabitees were not. Another similarity was the interviewees' limited identification with the women's liberation movement; only two called themselves feminists. The project's principal publications were two books, though neither made full use of Oakley's observational material, some of which proved too contentious to publish. The first of these books was published in 1979 as *Becoming a Mother* and under the different title *From Here to Maternity* when republished 2 years later and subsequently. Oakley repeated the formula used in *Housewife* of giving primacy to the interviewees' own words, here constituting most of the book. The organisation of the chapters took readers through the process sequentially, using excerpts of varying lengths from

the interview transcripts to tell the story from initial confir-
mation of pregnancy through preparation for motherhood
and the baby's birth to the various consequences of their
arrival for the mothers' lives. Dedicated to Adam, her own
first child, this book was followed by the publication in 1980
of *Women Confined*, a more conventional academic research
report that included quantitative as well as qualitative data
and engaged more extensively with scholarly debates.
Reflecting the different audience at which it was aimed, this
book included a much more extensive bibliography and an
index and theorised becoming a mother as a key social transition for women. She dedicated this book to her daughters,
Emily and Laura.

The two books complement each other as reports on
different aspects of the becoming a mother project. *From Here
to Maternity* conveys the joys and difficulties of motherhood
in the mothers' own words. Oakley responded to reviewers
who questioned the predominance of difficulties by pointing
out that prevailing myths did the opposite, accentuating the
positives. If the women's accounts highlighted problems, this
reflected their surprise at how much expectations and reality
diverged, especially where they had expected motherhood
would be the definitive expression of femininity. Recurrent
themes in the mothers' accounts were that becoming and
being a mother were not what they had imagined; first-hand
experience led them to regard popular images of motherhood
as romanticised. Recent contributions to the literature that
focused on the social origins of depression (including work by
her erstwhile PhD supervisor George Brown) as well as
Oakley's personal experiences prompted particular interest in
what women said about mental health. Several accounts
related to when the interviewees were still in hospital, the
average stay being nine days, and they supported Oakley's
theme of medicalisation's problematic impact. Preceding

decades had seen first babies in Great Britain born in hospital increase from 15% in 1927 to 99% in 1975. The greater sophistication of the medical technology available for hospital births had been offered as a justification of this, but some mothers' experience of childbirth was of medical staff paying more attention to what the technology was telling them than to what the mothers felt and said, with the result that the process was disempowering and less fulfilling than they had envisaged. Mills's notion of people finding themselves in situations resembling a series of traps applied here and also to the feelings of dependence on others and a lack of control reported by interviewees describing the effects of full-time motherhood having replaced employment. These women's lives were organised around their child's needs and characterised by waiting on a daily basis for their husbands to come home and over the longer term for their children to grow up so that they could return to paid work, as often as not after a decade out of the labour market.

The issue of mothers' mental health was pursued more extensively in *Women Confined* where Oakley treated difficulties reported in adjusting to motherhood as explicable by mothers' social situation rather than by hormones and other elements of the biological constitution of women's bodies. Oakley distinguished between postnatal blues, anxiety, depressed mood and depression and found that the incidence of these among her interviewees was, respectively, 84%, 71%, 33% and 24%. It was thus more common than not for the mothers to find themselves crying and upset and feeling anxious about their new situation, and quite common for them to report feeling low, sometimes being unable to function effectively. By treating these patterns as an understandable response on the part of many new mothers to their situation, including grieving for the loss of their former identity, Oakley identified becoming a mother as a major life transition that required significantly more adjustment than getting married did. It was therefore unfair to blame mothers who encountered difficulties for not making that adjustment smoothly. One factor in the transition to motherhood not going straightforwardly was the idealisation of motherhood; conversely, lesser concern with being the perfect mother was associated with more satisfactory outcomes. Even more striking was the connection found between the extent of obstetric intervention during the birth (as recorded in the patients' notes) and subsequent depression as reported in mothers' interviews. The association between the experience of childbirth as something over which they had little control and poor mental health outcomes for the mothers raised serious questions about medicalisation. A related finding associated vulnerability to poor mental health with mothers' lack of control over their lives more generally. Fourteen proposals were put forward in the book's conclusion, including greater social support with childcare being made available to parents by the state or community groups. Most of these recommendations were more grounded than those with which *Housewife* concluded, seeking to engage with various parties involved in having a baby besides the mothers: the medical profession, the hospital, the family and the state. Oakley also sought to contest anti-natalist strains in feminist thinking that treated motherhood as a burden best avoided.

Oakley developed several themes relating to policy-related debates about motherhood in various contributions to edited books. Written alone or with co-authors (including Robin Oakley, Hilary Graham, Iain Chalmers and Aidan Macfarlane), these chapters made diverse points: that the state did not treat marriage and parenthood as suitable for everyone, that official statisticians' focus exclusively on women's fertility revealed the presence of sexist assumptions, that social class influenced the extent to which reproduction was experienced as stressful, that the historical record showed medical science was important in specifying what constitutes a good mother and that the benefits claimed by professionals for medicalisation were contested by at least some of the recipients of their services. The history of the care received by pregnant women alerted Oakley to the opportunity to research archived materials relevant to claims about the steady accumulation of benefits brought by progress in scientific knowledge and medical practice. She suspected that this narrative was at best partial because it accorded high status to the knowledge of male medical experts and correspondingly downgraded wisdom that might be elicited from women, whether as mothers or midwives. Oakley's application to the Wellcome Trust for support was received so favourably that they offered her funding for a research fellowship lasting much longer than the period for which she had applied, and she spent the first three years of the 1980s analysing archive material and conducting interviews with key figures in the history of antenatal care, written up as *The Captured Womb*, published in 1984. The archives related to antenatal provision and maternity hospitals in Bristol, Edinburgh, Glasgow, London and Rochdale, and interviewees included Dugald Baird, whose pioneering work had been influenced by reading Richard Titmuss's 1943 book *Birth, Poverty and Wealth*. Oakley's inheritance of papers relating to the consequent correspondence and collaboration between Baird and her father serendipitously provided illuminating insights into the potential of debates between medical professionals and social scientists about social conditions and health outcomes, in this case relating to infant mortality. Baird was in his eighties when interviewed, and his recollections from a long career revealed the receptiveness of at least some medical professionals to sociological ideas.

Oakley's institutional base for working on *The Captured Womb* was the National Perinatal Epidemiological Unit at the Radcliffe Infirmary, Oxford, near to Somerville, her undergraduate college. The epidemiologist Iain Chalmers had established the unit in 1978. His openness to engagement with and learning from social scientists led Oakley to accept a consulting role there prior to her Wellcome award. Chalmers's interest in evidence-based medicine was associated with preparedness to question accepted wisdom, including about the policy conclusions drawn from research findings. Chalmers's advocacy of randomised controlled trials and of systematic reviewing prompted Oakley to reflect on the status of knowledge claims that informed debates about desirable reforms to maternity care. By the time *Women Confined* was published, she was questioning studies of women whose pregnancies had been classified as pathological in which researchers did not also include a control group of normal women. Her research into the history of medical care for pregnant women highlighted the patchiness of archival sources and reinforced her appreciation of open debate about research methods. At this time, the discussion of how best to proceed methodologically was mired in paradigm wars involving adversarial claims and counter claims about the prestige or opprobrium attached to rival ways of working. Oakley rejected having to choose between qualitative and quantitative approaches, preferring where appropriate to combine the two. Mixed methods informed the becoming a mother study's combination of observations, interviews and documentary analysis, while *The Captured Womb* reported on the analysis of archived documents and interviews. Writing *Subject Women*, Oakley's textbook for women's studies courses that she produced in a year taken away from primary research in the late 1970s, further confirmed the perversity of relying on only one type of data. It was axiomatic that articulating women's voices was necessary, but it was equally clear that demonstrating the extent of continuing gender inequalities in employment, education, health, domestic life, politics and many other areas is done most efficiently and effectively through the deployment of numbers. This methodological pluralism would stand her in good stead when it came to future research projects, including when returning to the topics of gender, housework and motherhood.

4

QUANTITATIVE AND QUALITATIVE METHODS

The unpredictability of audiences' receptiveness to a researcher's work is a common experience for academics, including Oakley. She was pleasantly surprised at the interest generated by *Sex, Gender and Society* (which is her second most-cited publication), while *Women Confined* and *Gender on Planet Earth* attracted less attention than she felt they merited. Regarding her publication which has been engaged with most often (as measured by citations), some readers misunderstood her purpose. This publication arose from the becoming a mother study and reflects on the practice of interviewing. Helen Roberts invited Oakley to write 'Interviewing women: a contradiction in terms?' for an edited collection on the nature of feminist research, a resource that was needed because research methods textbooks could leave novice researchers unprepared for the realities of data collection and analysis. Oakley broke with the convention that interviewers should decline to answer questions that interviewees put to them, doing so for both ethical and practical reasons. If people give up time to reveal things about their lives to interviewers, perhaps including intimate details (as was the case with the becoming a mother study), then it seems unfair to treat questions that they themselves might have as beyond the remit of the encounter, especially if those questions relate to basic facts about giving birth. Furthermore, interviews are social interactions that should be more like a conversation than an interrogation if interviewees are to feel at ease. The approach that treats the interviewer/interviewee relationship as hierarchical was for Oakley the embodiment of a masculine paradigm in which knowledge was extracted from subordinate research subjects. Her counter case was that interviewers who develop a more personal relationship with their research participants can feel reassured not only about behaving ethically but also about the quality of the data that they are collecting. The argument did not extend to asserting the blanket superiority of qualitative over quantitative methods that has sometimes been read into what Oakley wrote. Nor was Oakley seeking to equate feminist research with qualitative research, although some people supposed that she was, thereby confirming that a message intended is not necessarily a message received.

Misunderstandings of Oakley's intentions reflect the deleterious polarising effect of the paradigm warfare waged between advocates of quantitative and qualitative approaches to social science. Casual denigration of quantitative researchers as number-crunchers treated computer-aided analysis of statistical data sets as atheoretical and insensitive to what indicators actually measure; conversely, qualitative researchers were derided for lacking rigour, dealing impressionistically in anecdotes. The rival camps' partisan voices drowned out Howard Becker's pleas for tolerance of different approaches and warnings of the dangers of preaching a single right way of undertaking sociological investigation. Oakley's primary reliance on interviewing in the housework and becoming a mother studies led others to position her on the qualitative side of the putative methodological divide, despite *The Sociology of Housework* featuring tables using tests of significance and despite *Women*

Confined building its argument around a diagram that placed numerical values on the relationships between its component parts, demonstrating (for example) a correlation between extensive use of technology during childbirth and a mother's subsequent depression. Oakley had voiced various concerns about official statistics including the questionable ways in which concepts such as social class were operationalised, but she nevertheless appreciated their value in providing indications of unfolding social trends and drew on them extensively in *Subject Women* to capture shifts in gendered social inequality. Oakley's thinking about the status of the knowledge that different methods produced continued to develop. Immersion in archived sources for *The Captured Womb* led to engagement with Michel Foucault's ideas about the inseparability of power and knowledge. Her 1985 Introduction to *From Here to Maternity* argued that using women's own words registered not only the superiority of their expression compared to re-description by a sociologist – her original justification – but also declared that women's perspectives mattered and should not be silenced by medical professionals' habit of disregarding them. Analysing documentary evidence that control over childbirth had a long and contested history was creatively combined with working alongside Iain Chalmers's epidemiological team and prompted consideration of how sociologists might use experimental methods more usually associated with clinical trials to press for changes in perinatal practice. Oakley thus defied easy pigeon-holing as either qualitative or quantitative.

Oakley's openness to working alongside medical professionals facilitated the 1984 book *Miscarriage*, co-written with Ann McPherson, an Oxford General Practitioner with a particular interest in women's health, and Helen Roberts. Both Oakley and Roberts described themselves as medical sociologists, and all three authors brought personal experience to the project, having between them had five miscarriages as well as

seven children. This ratio of miscarriages to live births aligned
with their estimate of 426,000 miscarriages each year in Britain
compared to 640,000 births, although taboos surrounding the
topic made such estimation difficult. The book reported on a
questionnaire survey completed by 137 women with experience
of miscarriage, recruited through the National Association for
the Childless and the magazine *Mother and Baby* (which the
authors acknowledged was not a random sample). The information provided by these women was supplemented through a
survey of 20 GPs and 5 consultant obstetricians. These health
professionals provided accounts of treatment and advice that
indicated diversity of practice and echoed the experiences
reported by the women who had had miscarriages. Both parties
encountered difficulties when confronted with miscarriage,
exacerbated by a paucity of information about the subject and a
reluctance to discuss it which the book was intended to redress,
at least partially. It followed the style of *From Here to Maternity*,
quoting extensively from women's accounts. These reaffirmed
several themes from that study: that being pregnant is regarded
by prospective mothers as a major life event, that women often
felt not properly listened to by medical professionals (hospital
doctors, GPs and nurses featured much more frequently in the
lists of people identified as unhelpful than in the lists of helpful
people), and that women benefitted from alternative sources of
support and advice such as family and friends. The authors were
concerned less with academic analysis than with the provision of
useful information. Discussion was encouraged by noting, for
example, the sparsity of mentions of miscarriage in fictional
writing. Nevertheless, the practical suggestions made in its final
chapter (such as better provision of emotional support) aligned
with the proposals, offered in the spirit of sisterly solidarity, with
which *Women Confined* concluded. Oakley's book about midwives co-authored with Susanne Houd, *Helpers in Childbirth*,
also embodied this outlook.

Alongside these practical concerns regarding pregnant women's welfare, Oakley was also confronting more philosophical matters. *Subject Women* had been written for women's studies courses, raising the question of how these related to established disciplines, including sociology. She took the subversive step of re-classifying the component parts of women's lives so that discussions of women were not concentrated under the heading of marriage and the family and correspondingly neglected elsewhere. The book's organisation into six sections on citizenship, the making of a woman, labour, relationships, power and gender reflected themes important to women: their history of having inferior rights and status, how these inequalities are reproduced across the generations and through work (in all its forms), through relationships with others (including other women) and through the exercise of power. The concluding section assessed women's prospects of overcoming their oppression as a subordinate category of people. These discussions necessarily identified established sociologists' record of shortcomings in their analyses of women's position and how these emerged through problematic modes of enquiry. Talcott Parsons's influential argument that in families men undertook instrumental tasks and women expressive ones was, Oakley reasoned, the viewpoint of someone who must have had little personal experience of routine housework tasks that had nothing expressive about them, like washing floors and cleaning lavatories. Such misrepresentations arose from drawing sociological conclusions via grand theorising rather than evidence and experience. Other dangers lurked for sociologists who saw no place for emotions and feelings either in what they studied or in how they conducted their research. In addition to the case she had made previously about paying attention to women's subjective experiences, Oakley also argued that a researcher's own position as part of what they are studying meant that the scientific ideal of being value-neutral, of keeping their own views out of the research process, was an unachievable myth. A feminist sociology practised by researchers mindful of what brought them to their research topic was an appropriate way of improving women's lot. Moreover, because measured comparison with men's position is integral to doing this, quantitative as well as qualitative methods are needed when liberating sociology from its chauvinistic roots.

Taking stock of her life in her late thirties, Oakley contemplated various possible futures. She had already decided against teaching posts and knew that typically progression for researchers in male-dominated universities required the successful completion of relatively small-scale projects conducted independently to be followed in mid-career by larger grants which came with managerial roles involving oversight of and responsibility for other people. The alternative of remaining a contract researcher on a succession of fixed-term projects brought too much precariousness to contemplate as a long-term solution. Another option at this crossroads moment involved reviving the idea of becoming a novelist, prompted partly by descriptions of utopias found in feminist science fiction which provided imaginative ways of envisaging how the world might be reconfigured. *Subject Women* concluded with a brief discussion of this genre and references to it feature in other things that she wrote around this time, including some poetry. She later used the metaphor of a patchwork quilt to describe the combination of styles that she has employed in her writing about society; in her mind (if not necessarily the minds of all her readers), the contrasting parts constitute a coherent, colourful whole. Her decisions to take on greater administrative responsibilities by accepting the role of deputy director at the Thomas Coram Research Unit (TCRU), to extend the range of styles in which she wrote and to apply for a larger grant have more of a patchwork quality about them than a strategic career plan aiming at conventional markers of academic success. Nevertheless, in different ways, these things did provide two stimuli important to her: having an intellectual challenge, and a sense of contributing to improving women's well-being. The TCRU's mission of studying children's and families' social, educational and health needs fitted her interests, and she knew from personal correspondence received from numerous individual women who had read her work that it engaged audiences beyond academia. She envisaged that the larger grant would enable deeper exploration of social support for mothers-to-be which her previous research had identified as a significant lack, and her longstanding conversations with Chalmers convinced her to reconsider sociologists' antipathy towards experimental methods.

The story of Oakley's research into social support and pregnancy outcomes is long and complicated. Even the substantial book devoted to it, *Social Support and Motherhood*, provided only a partial account because a further round of data collection and several outputs came after its publication in 1992. Its genesis lay in two things: the observation that participants in the becoming a mother study reported benefitting from taking part, and debates among epidemiologists about the relative importance of medical and social interventions as influences on perinatal outcomes with which she had engaged when working with Chalmers and with the World Health Organization (WHO) and in her historical research for *The Captured Womb*. If Oakley's ambitions for her becoming a mother study went well beyond those that had motivated her housework research, the social support and pregnancy outcomes study took this ratcheting up of ambition further still. Oakley's aims included promoting interdisciplinary dialogue between social and medical scientists. Mutual suspicion and propensity to work to different agendas bedevilled researchers at the interface between social science and medicine, but Oakley's time at the National Perinatal Epidemiological Unit had involved productive dialogues, for example, about the relevance of social class to the stress experienced during pregnancy and childbirth-related problems associated with it such as low birth weight. Babies born under 2500 g (approximately 5.5 pounds) were twice as common among mothers in social class V compared to social class I mothers. Further correlations existed between lower social class and higher rates of stillbirth, maternal mortality, and babies born with disabilities such as oral clefts. Clearly, sociologists could add something to debates about problems associated with reproduction, and learn something from medical scientists about the physiological mechanisms by which social class disadvantage translates into bodily outcomes. A second project aim involved using methodological tools which medical scientists respected and used frequently, notably randomised controlled trials, the results of which were more trustworthy than those of trials without a randomised comparison. Medical scientists could be dismissive of qualitative methods for being soft (that is, lacking rigour). Generating results using an approach prized as a gold standard because of its capacity to overcome the problem of findings being influenced by extraneous factors would be harder to disregard.

Oakley's ambitiousness inevitably carried risks. Projects involving enough participants to run a large-scale randomised controlled trial are both challenging to organise and expensive. The final research sites for which ethics approval was secured were, in terms of socio-economic profiles, very different places in England (Berkshire, Derby, Stoke-on-Trent and Tunbridge Wells). Associated with each participating hospital, a dedicated research midwife was funded part-time.

Oakley held monthly face-to-face meetings in London with these four midwives (who were, incidentally, all mothers themselves) and the project co-ordinator (Lyn Rajan) and secretary (Sandra Stone) to aid the study's coherence. In addition to its complex research architecture, approaching such a project with the explicit intention of contributing to both medical and social science risked research funders that specialise in one or other field considering the application beyond their purview, which did indeed happen. Referees' comments that embodied disciplinary partisanship regarding research design contributed to this outcome. The project went ahead only through a combination of funding sources (principally the then Department of Health and Social Security, along with the ESRC, the Iolanthe Trust and the Institute of Education Research Fund), drawn on at different, sometimes overlapping, periods of time. During the early stages there was no certainty that the planned intervention would be supported. A further risk was that the experimental method required the identification of measurable variables that would be acceptable to both medical and social scientists as indicators of the success or otherwise of the planned intervention in the lives of pregnant women. Eventually Oakley settled on social support as the independent variable, and hypotheses were built around 15 dependent variables, most crucially the baby's birthweight, in relation to which the working hypothesis was that provision of better social support to women during pregnancy would increase the babies' mean birthweight. All 509 mothers-to-be who agreed to participate in the study had previously had a low birthweight baby, and they were allocated randomly to either the intervention group or the control group. After extensive preparations and piloting, the trial began early in 1986.

The study findings confirmed that women's experience of pregnancy can be enhanced through social support. In Oakley's

becoming a mother study, the social support that the prospective
mothers appreciated had come directly from her, an outsider to
medical and health professions. The employment of midwives as
the researchers providing direct support to the women in the
social support and pregnancy outcomes project might have led
to a different effect had the women's responses been shaped by
their proffered support coming from people who had undergone
recognised midwifery training, but the results indicated that
receiving social support from someone with formal training was
perfectly acceptable to the participants, coming as it did sepa-
rately from standard ante-natal care. It was crucial that the
research midwives avoided any semblance of surveillance when
providing their support, for example being careful to eschew
judgemental comments about the women's lifestyles. The
amount of support that women in the intervention group
received was relatively modest, but even three home visits at 14,
20 and 28 weeks into the pregnancy together with two telephone
calls or brief visits between these dates and the opportunity for
the women to get in touch with the research midwife by telephone at any time were effective in securing an improvement in
outcomes (relative to those of the control group) according to
several measures of mothers' health and well-being, such as
lower incidence of depression during pregnancy. Because the
study sample comprised women who had previously had a low
birthweight baby and because the rates of having a low birthweight baby are higher among women occupying lower social
class positions, the research midwives frequently encountered
women in positions of socio-economic disadvantage such as
poverty and poor housing. The sense of humour that Oakley had
specified as one of the prerequisites of the research midwife role
lightened the tone of some interactions with the women in the
study, for example, when one of them jokily likened her con-
voluted family network to those created for dramatic effect by
television soap opera scriptwriters, but on other occasions the

harsh realities of social deprivation dispelled any feelings of levity.

By a curious coincidence, the issue of *New Society* in which Oakley's very first article appeared in 1970 also included a celebrated contribution from Basil Bernstein which argued that offsetting the consequences of wider social inequalities among children would be hard to achieve through school-based initiatives alone. Oakley became a colleague of Bernstein's at the Institute of Education when she joined the TCRU, and his message that education cannot compensate for society, that social inequalities run sufficiently deep to hamper the construction of effective policy interventions, relates to the same conundrum that Oakley's project team encountered. With few material resources at their disposal, it was beyond the research midwives' power to take the project participants away from substandard accommodation or the pressures of managing on low and erratic incomes. Notwithstanding these durable social structural constraints, however, the research midwives were recognised as having been very or particularly helpful by half of the women and quite helpful by a further 44%, leaving only a small number reporting nothing positive about the information provision, advice, referrals to other support available and general preparedness to listen that the research midwives offered. Quite simply, the research midwives were valued as people who showed concern about the women's everyday lives, taking an interest in their situation and offering considered advice when asked to, as part of giving them time and attention. The longest chapter in *Social Support and Motherhood* is comprised of detailed accounts of the lives of four women, predominantly in their own words together with insights into their situations that the research midwives had gained. Each research area contributed one case study, further confirming that each of the research midwives was able to build supportive relationships with the research participants. In some instances this was in tension with elements of their professional training, for example in relation to smoking during pregnancy; experts associate this with low birthweight but not all women who smoked were prepared to countenance cessation. For women who experience life as a trap from which it is hard to escape, smoking offers a way of managing their stress levels, as the research midwives, being supportive, had to acknowledge.

The small superiority in the mean birthweight of babies in the intervention part of the trial compared to that of the control group was insufficient to establish a statistically significant influence of social support provided to the mothers. Oakley accepted that she had been overambitious to expect the babies of the mothers in receipt of social support from the research midwives would show an increase of 150 g compared to the control group figure but pointed to outcomes measured by other variables (such as lower rates of Caesarean sections) as evidence that pregnant women had benefitted from the social support provided. As with her previous research, historical material was used to show how understanding of the phenomenon being investigated had evolved. In the 18th century average birthweight figures of 10–16 lb (4500–7500 g) were reported, but these serious overestimates were merely guesswork. As data based on systematic observations become more widely available, patterns of measurement still varied according to how weights were collected, who was responsible for collecting them, and how soon after the birth the data collection occurred. Culture mattered here as well as technology, for example through the superstition that weighing a baby might result in its death, or through the influence of insurance schemes in which payment depended on a minimum weight being reached in cases of stillbirth, a situation that applied in Greece, Oakley noted. She had acquired extensive knowledge of comparative data and was aware of the variability characterising their collection (and hence their accuracy) through her work on perinatal services for the WHO, later published in *Helpers in Childbirth*. This made her wary of some of the arguments that she encountered, but also introduced her to the imagination that underpinned various innovative interventions, such as the Guatemalan initiative that teamed up pregnant women with untrained female companions for the duration of their labour (which proved successful). This WHO work highlighted the differences of writing reports for audiences looking for policy recommendations, which involve a contrasting style to academic sociology. The format of refereed articles in medical journals was different again, being shorter and more focused on quantitative findings than she had been used to.

The social support and pregnancy outcomes project left Oakley mulling over audiences' receptivity to the presentation of findings. This can vary with which publications they read. Doctors are more likely than sociologists to read articles like the one that she, Lynda Rajan and Adrian Grant had published in the *British Journal of Obstetrics and Gynaecology* (which followed the format of concentrating on statistical findings). The converse held for her articles in *Sociology* (also with Rajan) and *Sociology of Health and Illness*; being longer, they allowed more space for qualitative material alongside the numbers. In addition to selectivity regarding which journals people routinely read, there are issues about the types of material with which readers feel comfortable. In a provocative formulation, Oakley's article in *Women and Health* was entitled 'Who's afraid of the randomised controlled trial?'. Her discussion of concerns about ethics (such as whether trials deny participants control over their involvement and limit their informed consent) and about uncertainty argued spiritedly against outright rejection of the approach. Medical experimentation had acquired a tarnished reputation through the unethical practices of doctors at Auschwitz, Tuskegee and elsewhere, but such episodes did not make experimentation inherently problematic; regulatory safeguards can and should be put in place to prevent abuse. Done well, experimentation can inform assessments of policy interventions, in some cases casting doubt on long-established practices that are asserted without evidence to be effective. Oakley used a study of interventions with young people dating back to when her mother had been a social worker to note that efforts to reduce delinquency had been associated with increased rather than decreased problems. However uncomfortable it is to have one's preconceptions questioned, research findings that go against expectations are valuable because they require revised explanations, thereby acting as stimuli to theoretical advances. The history of pregnant women's care had taught Oakley that not all benefits claimed for innovations stood up to scrutiny when tested against the evidence, even where the logic proffered for making the change seemed incontrovertible. Medical professionals schooled in particular ways of working were unlikely to be receptive to the systematic questioning of their practice that Oakley's argument implied, nor favourably predisposed to her view that medical services provided for mothers remained largely unevaluated.

Oakley's chosen title for a collection of essays, lectures and poems published in 1986, *Telling the Truth about Jerusalem*, was not appreciated by all her readers, she later recounted. Her reason for referring to William Blake's poem Jerusalem was that the subsequent adoption of its musical rendition as a celebration of women gaining the right to vote masked a complicated and troubling history because Millicent Fawcett embraced not only feminism but also nationalism and imperialism. This was merely one example of how feminists forget their movement's history at their peril. Expressed more positively, history when it is faithfully recorded has many lessons to impart to subsequent generations. Oakley was mindful that first wave feminism had been marked by divisions and disagreements just as second wave feminism was. There are many versions of Jerusalem, the ideal society for which people strive, and Oakley had sought to convey how this applied to feminists when, in *Subject Women*, she described 10 rival tendencies in the women's liberation movement. Oakley's broad characterisation of herself as engaged in the promotion of feminist social science led her not only to question malestream approaches but also into conflict with feminists who held different views about theorising and about methodology. Her critique of Parsons's penchant for operating with contrasting pairs of concepts (such as treating men's role in families as instrumental and women's as expressive) was extended to dichotomous thinking more generally. Her conclusion was that either/or thinking imposed a straitjacket when what was needed was openness and creativity. In this, Oakley had much in common with other feminist responses to masculine or masculinist social science's in-built biases, but she found herself at odds with those writers who developed theoretical concepts such as patriarchy in opaque language that was difficult to incorporate into empirical investigations, and with others who drew the conclusion that feminist research had no place for quantitative methods. Neither theory-building detached from empirical research nor non-engagement with numbers could adequately address the persistent pattern of one in 15 babies born in Britain weighing less than 5 ½ lb and suffering various adverse health statuses as a result.

Feminists who eschewed quantitative methods were criticised by Oakley for paying insufficient attention to the lessons of history. Campaigns for social reform waged by key historical figures such as Jane Addams, Harriet Martineau, Florence Nightingale and Beatrice Webb had all benefitted from statistical evidence about the poverty and inequality from which women suffered disproportionately. Statistical data were also collected by 19th-century feminists to reveal women's routine exclusion from research positions and the adverse consequences that this had on the quality of the knowledge produced by male scientists whose gendered biases masqueraded as objective truth when discussing subjects such as women's supposedly inferior intelligence. The argument advanced by some of Oakley's contemporaries that feminist research required qualitative methods led her to ask how this gendering of methodology had come about. Feminists' critique of positivism figured prominently in this story, and Oakley's depiction of Auguste Comte, the founding father of sociology, as a doctrinaire sexist may have contributed to this, since the term positivism was coined by him to describe his philosophy. Feminists were among those who contested Comte's positivistic belief in laws of social development that could be discovered by science; such a view was too mechanistic to allow for active intervention to re-shape politics and women's place in society. Positivism's concern with orderly predictability was too fateful in its denial of agency, and it disregarded women's alternative visions of the future. In addition, positivism was criticised for the rigid, formulaic and exploitative way in which its practitioners acquired knowledge regardless of the effect this had on research subjects, to which a parallel was drawn with rape. Shulamit Reinharz was one author who drew this parallel, based in part in her own unhappy experiences as a junior researcher working on a survey project which was manipulative and unethical as well as failing to get at how participants understood the world. Some of these criticisms resonated with points Oakley had made about the shortcomings of conventional interviewing, but it seemed unnecessarily restrictive to Oakley to reject the use of quantitative methods altogether, believing as she did that there was nothing inherently in conflict with feminist values in using them.

Looking back now to the period when paradigm warfare was at its fiercest can leave one wondering why there was so much contention. Oakley was an early exponent of mixed methods research before that term became widely used, as was her TCRU colleague Julia Brannen. Oakley's integration of quantitative and qualitative methods in the social support and pregnancy outcomes study was particularly innovative through combining qualitative interviewing and a randomised controlled trial. Things subsequently moved so quickly that an exchange in *Sociology* in 2004 between Oakley and Gayle Letherby, one of a younger generation of feminists, revealed little disagreement about the benefits of mixing methods, only different perspectives on how recently feminists had by and large become comfortable combining quoting and counting, in the process moving away from the idea that a particular method might be intrinsically feminist. Elsewhere, Oakley went further in arguing that the distinction between qualitative and quantitative methods was overplayed and becoming redundant, noting that the observer's position affects not only those working with qualitative data but also quantitative data users' perceptions; passion, intuition and imagination feature in their discoveries as well as the careful testing of hypotheses. Choices about methods should be driven by the research question being pursued, Oakley argued, and when making these choices, issues such as validity and bias need to be heeded whatever the methods under consideration. Her concern for researchers to be open about their biases was evident early on when she quoted approvingly Charles Wright Mills's views on the subject in *The Sociology of Housework*, and she remained alert to biases being hidden in apparently innocuous formulations. This could happen, for example, in the operationalisation of concepts. In the social support and pregnancy outcomes study, the concept of social support was rightly seen as preferable to the vague and inescapably normative concept of community which Oakley knew from her reading of community studies to be hard to capture. She drew attention, however, to the fact that some recipients of social support experienced it more as a burden than a benefit, indicating therefore that it should not be regarded as unambiguously positive in all cases, as the research went on to confirm.

Like 'community', the concept of 'family' suffered problems of imprecision and association with idealised social arrangements, and when Oakley's attention turned to young people's health, it was the households in which they lived that provided the focus of the analysis, not their broader family and kinship relationships. Although the book reporting on the study was entitled *Young People, Health and Family Life*, the term household better captured the young people's home lives because more than a quarter of the 843 young people in their mid-teens who participated in the survey did not live with both biological parents, and the same applied to the young people who participated in the interview part of the study. This and the multiplicity of other domestic arrangements (including living with lone mothers, lone fathers, in step-families or in other configurations that reflected the sample's multi-ethnic character) meant that the powerful cultural notion of a normal family was misleading, and household diversity provided a more satisfactory analytical framework. The study involved Oakley in a team based at TCRU that included Brannen (whose previous research shared many of her substantive interests as well as her concerns to develop mixed methods) along with Kathryn Dodd and Pamela Storey and it continued into Oakley's period as Director of the Social Science Research Unit. The research design represented a point of departure for Oakley in that the sample was not comprised only or primarily of women; boys outnumbered girls among the young people in the survey element of the project and the 56 in the interview stage, although fathers constituted only 36% of the 86 parents prepared to be interviewed. Oakley's interviews with fathers proved noticeably briefer and less reflective than those with mothers and consequently provided fewer insights for the research team. Nevertheless, their terseness further confirmed what other participants said about mothers having primary responsibility for their teenage children's health and well-being, and about young people's relationships with their mothers being closer than those they had with their fathers. These findings were unsurprising to the research team, given that previous projects of theirs had highlighted mothers' centrality to family life and household management, though the inclusion of other voices reinforced this conclusion.

The value of the project's mixed-methods design, combining a survey with interviews, was demonstrated by the complementarity of the two sets of findings which provided more depth of understanding than each on its own would have done. Challenges of following this approach were also revealed. The 142 interviewees were drawn either from among the young people who had been part of the survey of west London schoolchildren or were parents of a survey participant, but there was a time lag of 6–15 months between the survey's completion by 15 or 16-year-olds still in full-time education and the interviews being conducted. By this time, some of the young people had entered employment and (potentially at least) all had matured in their outlook. Discrepancies between young people's survey and interview responses therefore had to be treated with caution because they may have been attributable to changed circumstances or outlooks, or they may have reflected the capacity of different research instruments to prompt inconsistent answers. This can happen, for example, if research participants are more comfortable with the impersonality of surveys than face-to-face interviews when discussing sensitive matters. One young woman made no mention when interviewed of the suicide attempt that had been revealed in her survey answers. The rarity of such discrepancies meant that the project team could nevertheless be confident that almost half of the young people engaged in none of the risk-related behaviours asked about of alcohol consumption, smoking and drug-taking. The stereotype of rebellious teenagers was also contradicted by most young people reporting good relations with their parents. Furthermore, young people were more disapproving than their parents of behaviour that carried health risks, casting doubt on the cultural construction of teenagers' behaviour as a social problem. That said, the study's conclusion that the transfer of responsibility for health from parents to young people is a difficult and erratic process that is incomplete as they enter adulthood has important implications for strategies of health education. In addition, as things stood at the time, policies spoke too much to young people as undifferentiated individuals, and too little to the specificities of their gender, ethnicity and social class.

The *Young People, Health and Family Life* study extended beyond Oakley's time at TCRU, publication coming four years into her SSRU role which commenced in 1990. Parents' observations in the study about their children being less radical than they had been in their youth resonated with the view expressed by some young women that gender equality had been achieved. In the mid-1980s, the second collection that Oakley co-edited with Juliet Mitchell identified *What is Feminism?* as a timely but deceptively difficult question to answer as awareness grew of differences between women both materially and in their political stances, not least as they contemplated feminism's achievements. Mitchell and Oakley posed the awkward question of whether feminism meant a concern with women's position or required a focus on human welfare more broadly, including that of men.

Oakley's alignment with the latter position led her to argue that when feminist researchers restricted their attention to women, they opened themselves up to criticisms like those previously levelled at studies involving only male participants. The 38th publication from the social support and pregnancy outcomes study asked whether the presence of men in households improved the welfare of women and children, and while these data about household members were derived solely from mothers, the inclusion of questions about men allowed conclusions to be drawn about the mixed blessings that fathers in conventional nuclear families brought. Oakley and her co-author Alan Rigby (a statistician interested in children's health) showed that the material benefits of greater economic security brought by fathers had to be balanced against the emotional stresses that often accompanied their presence. Tellingly, the more diverse sample of fathers in the *Young People, Health and Family Life* study were also typically reliant on the emotional labour that their partners put into routine family relationships, as several conceded in their interviews. This theme also appeared in Oakley's novels in which parenting of teenage children featured, notably *The Men's Room*, *Only Angels Forget*, *The Secret Lives of Eleanor Jenkinson* and *A Proper Holiday*.

In *Taking It Like a Woman*, Oakley declared that being a feminist meant putting women first, but observed that the problem to be addressed needed to be not women and their behaviour but men and theirs. This lay at the root of women's second-class status and constituted the principal obstacle to overcoming gender inequality. Her arguments about women being more attuned than men to emotional aspects of life identify a fundamental challenge to understanding men. The fieldwork for *Young People, Health and Family Life* showed that while interviewing women may present difficulties, interviewing men had the capacity to generate challenges of a different order. In this study, the fathers showed greater reluctance to be interviewed, and interviews with those who did agree were characterised by a terseness that was not attributable to the research team being all female since male interviewers on other projects reported similar experiences. It followed that alternative research methods would be needed as vehicles for improving the quality of data being collected. Oakley noted that feminist researchers had extended the research methods deployed to good effect, citing Janet Finch's use of vignettes and Hilary Graham's use of storytelling. She observed approvingly that male sociologists who were drawing inspiration from developments in women's studies to pioneer the emerging field of men's studies were making similarly adventurous methodological choices. Such innovation did not have to entail devising wholly new methods, as her own experimentation with randomised controlled trials had shown; employing this method might be unfamiliar to sociologists, but it was so much part of normal science for medical researchers that one in 10 patients in Britain in the mid-1980s were participating in a trial (not always knowingly). Oakley's openness to experimenting with methods reflected her preference for methodological pluralism over paradigm warfare. She recognised that telling a story can be done using various formats, with correspondingly different ways of knowing. She nevertheless bemoaned the lack of detail provided by many researchers about the conduct of their investigations because without such information it is hard to assess the quality of the findings. This theme grew in importance as she became more deeply engaged with systematic reviewing.

5

POLICY RELEVANCE AND ACCUMULATED KNOWLEDGE

Oakley regarded the ladder-like imagery associated with conventional academic career progression as more suited to men's lives than to women's. She preferred the alternative idea of a patchwork quilt comprising diverse and contrasting elements that constitute an attractive, patterned whole which requires skill and dedication to create. It allows for revisited themes and addition of new material. The year 1990 saw significant shifts for Oakley, both personally and professionally. In *Father and Daughter*, she recounted how, coinciding with the menopause, she felt compelled to leave the Thomas Coram Research Unit. In these unpropitious circumstances, she founded the Social Science Research Unit. Various investigations begun in the 1980s (such as the social support and pregnancy outcomes project and the *Young People, Health and Family Life* study) highlighted the need for better evidence through systematic reviewing of existing literature in diverse fields of policy-relevant social science. Her new position facilitated pursuit of this theme in numerous areas, working with a team that started small but expanded rapidly following the foundation in 1995 of the Centre for the Evaluation of

Health Promotion and Social Interventions, subsequently renamed the Evidence-Informed Policy and Practice Information and Coordinating Centre (or EPPI Centre for short). Early funding for this initiative came from the Department of Health, which had supported several previous projects of Oakley's, including parts of the social support and pregnancy outcomes study and the investigation of young people's health with Julia Brannen and other colleagues. Her vision for the Social Science Research Unit (SSRU) was nevertheless broader than an exclusive focus on health matters, which anyway she knew to be impossible to separate from family, educational and other social influences. Oakley also promoted methodological innovation at SSRU, one example of which was her and Gillian Bendelow's use of drawing to explore 9–10-year-olds' knowledge of and beliefs about cancer. Oakley's 15 years as SSRU Director were remarkably productive in terms of research grants, publications and other achievements. By 2005, she had passed the then retirement age of 60, although retiring from the role did not mean retirement from academic work, merely from academic management. A continuing link to SSRU as Founding Director remained prominent among many ongoing activities. She chose Professor of Sociology and Social Policy as the title of the personal chair to which she was promoted in 1991, indicating her concerns with policy relevance at a time when postmodernists were seeking to steer sociology in a quite different direction to that of policy evaluation.

Oakley's interest in evaluation was in a way already well established. Her concern to evaluate feminism's achievements dated from the 1970s, when housewives in her PhD study questioned what difference feminism had made or might make. First wave feminism's success in securing women's right to vote was recognised as a necessary but not a sufficient condition for achieving women's equality to men, thus necessitating evaluation of progress towards other objectives. Although not a formal evaluation, *Subject Women* included the stock-taking exercise of judging how much things had changed by the start of the 1980s and what still needed to happen to overcome women's subordination and oppression. By 1986, when *What is Feminism?* (the second collection co-edited with Juliet Mitchell) appeared, the evaluative task had expanded to cover not only the progress made towards gender equality but also the impact of the backlash against feminism. This theme grew in importance over the ensuing decade to become the main focus of Mitchell and Oakley's third collection, *Who's Afraid of Feminism?* Not only was it important to record the achievements of feminists in terms of legislation outlawing sex discrimination in workplaces and enshrining reproductive rights, for example, it was also necessary to highlight the tasks that remained. Over-optimistic assessments that the key injustices had been addressed needed to be contested, as did hostile arguments that feminism had produced undesirable unintended consequences that diluted the case for further change and even raised the prospect of reversing the changes achieved. Later, while reviewing how things stood in the year 2000, Oakley reflected on people declaring themselves sick to death of hearing about women's issues. Arguments that feminism does not work in practice have long been a predictable response to feminist critiques of familiar institutions. Oakley produced one such critique of conventional families in a 1982 chapter in which claims that families were functional for the wider society, that they 'worked', were questioned on the grounds that evidence from studies of marital satisfaction and statistics on the rising incidence of divorce suggested otherwise. Whether something works is an empirical question requiring careful assessment of evidence. Oakley's assessment was that social changes including the growth of married women's employment and the spread of feminist ideas were placing increasing strains on the routine operation of conventional families.

Oakley's perspective on families echoed Charles Wright Mills's discussion in *The Sociological Imagination* of the fact that a quarter of American marriages were ending in divorce within 4 years. Illustrating perfectly his proposition that personal troubles are also public issues, it showed too sociologists' capacity to use first-hand experience: Mills himself figured in those statistics. Comparable statistics for Britain were lower, but the point still held that rosy myths surrounding marriage and conventional family life could lead to personal unhappiness. Oakley's experiences of frustration with the housewife role and of postnatal depression indicated that she was, like Mills, not immune to such dissatisfaction. Several chapters of *Taking It Like A Woman* were devoted to dissecting the shortcomings of marriage and the family as institutions into which she and Robin tried to fit themselves and their children, in the process experiencing the downsides of conformity to social norms and the pursuit of unachievable patriarchal ideals. The shortcomings of marriage had been sufficient to lead Oakley to argue in *Housewife* for the abolition not only of the housewife role but also of the family, although a decade later, she was noting that despite divorce rates reaching seemingly epidemic proportions, individual divorces were typically followed by remarriage. Family relationships bring both reward and infuriation, albeit men and women report this in different ways. The contradictoriness of family relationships also ran through *Man and Wife*, her account of her parents' marriage which had been solemnised when gendered expectations were less contested than they became for Oakley's generation. In both cases, Mills's observation applied about people experiencing their lives as traps into which they had fallen, although by 2000, the year Oakley published *Experiments in Knowing*, her enthusiasm for

Mills's encouragement to exercise the sociological imagination was tempered by frustration with his penchant for making rhetorically powerful statements without providing sufficient justification in terms of supporting evidence. After devoting much thought to the methodological foundations of robust evaluation, Oakley's list of questions to ask when evaluating something was extensive and testing, and she lamented the frequency with which researchers failed to demonstrate that good grounds existed for readers to accept their analyses.

The argument that welfare service provision is based more on service providers' beliefs about the best way of proceeding than it is on rigorous assessment of evidence about the most effective means of meeting clients' wishes had first been advanced by Oakley in relation to health professionals' treatment of pregnant women. Investigation of further topics showed this to be a more general phenomenon. Busy professionals may assume that their established patterns of working are the most appropriate, but Oakley concluded that the doctors encountered by women during their pregnancies and motherhood could also exhibit an ideological attachment to their favoured practices which they sustained even if compelling research findings suggested otherwise. Her SSRU work revealed that this problem was not restricted to medical professionals; indeed, it was quite possibly more pronounced among professionals in the fields of education and social work, thereby raising important questions about the efficacy of and the underlying justifications provided for efforts to improve people's welfare generally. A good example of Oakley's evaluation of interventions related to sex education for young people. Building on findings from the *Young People, Health and Family Life* study about how adolescents take on responsibility for their health and well-being, Oakley and Deirdre Fullerton, Janet Holland, Sean Arnold, Merry France-Dawson, Peter Kelley and Sheena

McGrellis (all SSRU colleagues) subjected the literature on sexual health interventions aimed at young people to systematic review. Oakley knew from the study that she and colleagues had conducted in west London that young people had varying degrees of interest in and awareness of sexual health issues but also a disturbing propensity to take risks in relation to pregnancy and sexually transmitted infections. By the mid-1990s, when the systematic review was undertaken, the material considered included reports on initiatives prompted by HIV/AIDS, about which there was understandable interest regarding their effectiveness in counteracting the spread of the disease: almost half of the literature they concentrated on had this as its specific focus. Discovering ways not only of educating young people regarding HIV/AIDS but also of promoting behaviour change (which knowledge acquisition on its own did not necessarily bring about) were urgent policy objectives at that time.

Oakley and her colleagues were part of a broad movement promoting systematic reviews as a way of bringing rigour to the analysis of what is already known about an issue by examining the bases on which relevant studies were conducted. Oakley's experience with randomised controlled trials in the social support and pregnancy outcomes study led her to pay particular attention to the way in which research participants were allocated to either the intervention or the control group, but the literature on policy interventions in the field of sex education for young people was not always clear on how this had been done in the studies being reported. Some cases even lacked clarity over the basic issue of whether a control group had been used to provide a point of comparison with the group receiving the intervention. Across eight criteria for judging the methodological soundness of the research design of the 65 projects subjected to detailed consideration, only 54% met five or more and only 6% met all eight. These were surprisingly low figures that undermined confidence in the rigour of the broad body of research, even allowing for the fact that some of the projects deemed unsound (which constituted 82% of the projects considered) were judged so because they had not provided sufficient information about how the research had been undertaken to give the assessors confidence in their diligence. Thus, for example, the absence of information about the situation prior to an intervention or after it undermines confidence in claims made about the effectiveness or otherwise of that intervention; this was the case in 68% and 59%, respectively, of the studies reviewed. Each study was assessed by at least two members of the reviewing team because assessments of methodological rigour can vary. Where disagreement occurred, at least one further team member added their assessments before consensus was reached. The methodological flaws and limitations identified by the reviewers led them to be more cautious than the authors of the published papers reviewed typically were when making claims about the effectiveness or otherwise of interventions. In one case, the reviewers judged an intervention decidedly harmful because it resulted in an increase in behaviour deemed undesirable, the precise opposite of what had been intended.

The study of interventions relating to young people's sex education raised issues that Oakley and her colleagues came to regard as common features of systematic reviewing generally through investigating other topics. Oakley's openness about her own methodological practice (for example, by including interview schedules in publications) turned out not to be standard practice. Lack of transparency not only made the evaluation of projects difficult; it also stood as a barrier to knowledge becoming cumulative, not least because replication of studies was made difficult. A further problem related to publication bias, whereby projects deemed successful are more likely to be reported on than ones judged by researchers to have failed, even though there are important lessons to be learned from all studies, failures as well as successes. In addition, the context in which the research was undertaken must be considered. In the study of sex education for young people, over 90% of the literature originated from North America; almost all the rest came from the United Kingdom and other European countries. Making allowances for contrasting national policy contexts presents a challenge when synthesising research findings. A related problem concerns the timing of studies included in a systematic review. In the case of the study of young people's sex education, initially publications were included that had come out in the years 1982–1994, but some earlier studies were added that had come to light via the bibliographies of the initial selection. Questions of research ethics also figure in the process of systematic review. Oakley had long been familiar with the view that it is unethical to deny participants allocated to control groups access to interventions that are potentially of benefit to them. She disagreed with this position because randomised trials require such control groups to be effective and because interventions may be harmful. There were other issues encountered through systematic reviewing that rang alarm bells regarding unethical procedures. Some of these related to matters of confidentiality and anonymity, some to how the informed consent of participants was obtained and some to questions of whether resources used up in research projects were justified, including in those calculations not wasting participants' time.

Criticisms of others' research will tend to be better informed and as a result more readily accepted if the critics themselves have first-hand experience of undertaking data collection and analysis. Oakley and colleagues from collaborating institutions illustrated the value of learning by doing through insights gained from their investigation of sex education in schools. In this study, known as the Randomised Intervention of Pupil Peer-led Sex Education (RIPPLE) study, 29 participating schools from across southern and central England were randomly allocated either to be given the intervention or to be part of the control in which no changes to the sex education curriculum were made (15 and 14 schools, respectively); one from each group subsequently dropped out, leaving 27 schools. The project's ambitious design employed qualitative methods (such as interviews and researcher fieldnotes) within the experimental framework. The project was ambitious not only because of this unusual combination of methods but also due to the innovation of encouraging the active involvement of participants in shaping the research process. The project's working hypothesis was that sex education will be more effectively delivered to schoolchildren by their peers than by teachers, an idea explored by training year 12 students aged 16–17 who had volunteered to lead sessions on sex education in school time with groups of year nine students, only 3 years their junior. The intervention provided information about and opportunities to discuss sexual relationships, sexually transmitted diseases and contraception. It used questionnaires to gauge students' knowledge, attitudes and behaviour after 6 months, two years and into the longer term, by which time it was considered appropriate to include pregnancy rates among the variables investigated. Unlike the *Young People, Health and Family Life* study, the project excluded independent and single-sex schools, and fewer than 10% of the 343 mixed-sex comprehensive state schools approached ended up taking part. Some were excluded because they declined to participate without guaranteed inclusion among those implementing the peer-led sex education, which went against trials' requirement of a control group to which potential participants are allocated randomly. Nevertheless, those participating were broadly representative of state schools in England and sufficient to generate access to 8,766 young people in two cohorts and some 130 staff.

The representativeness of the participating schools and their random allocation to the intervention or control groups mattered because the experiment was designed to produce findings relevant to the policy objectives of reducing the rates of unprotected sexual intercourse, sexually transmitted infections and unintended teenage pregnancies and terminations, along with the broader goal of improving the quality of sexual relationships. The selection of schools took into account their heterogeneity according to factors such as pupils' socio-economic and ethnic profiles, their rural/urban location and their educational attainment, all plausible influences on the risk of teenage pregnancy. Research team members worked in contexts which were diverse in further ways, such as school size, patterns of timetable organisation and curriculum delivery, classroom cultures and the degree of teachers' enthusiasm for the project. Because these were not uniform conditions, the researchers needed to be flexible about how the peer-led sex education was delivered and how data gathering through the completion of questionnaires was conducted. The research team could not control the amount of time allocated for pupils to complete questionnaires, for example, and (predictably) completion rates were lower in those schools where the task was allocated less time. The use of researcher fieldnotes in the project facilitated the whole team's reflections on the survey data that were collected. Three fieldworkers managed the peer-educator training, observed the sessions in which the students completed the survey and the focus groups in which participants' experiences of taking part in the project were discussed. They were able to share their notes with each other and with the wider project team just as the research midwives had in Oakley's social support and pregnancy outcomes study. Compared to that study, the RIPPLE project team was larger and more multidisciplinary, and the mixed methods research design prompted useful discussion among team members of how research methods choices have a bearing not only on the nature of the data gathered but also on the process of their interpretation. Fieldworkers' participation in casual conversations during the fieldwork and their observation of related incidents helped to sensitise the research team to alternative understandings of what the findings might mean.

Interest in the potential of peer-led sex education in schools to reduce unwanted teenage pregnancies reflected UK rates of teenage pregnancy being the highest in Europe. The fact that 5% of the young women in the study had had an abortion by the age of 20 gave some indication of the scale of the challenge, but this figure was the same for both intervention and control group schools, thereby dashing hopes the intervention might be associated with a long-term reduction. Other studies had led the research team to expect the control group's abortion rate to be closer to 9%, making them conscious of the incompleteness of data collected several years on from the intervention with 13- and 14-year-olds. Keeping track of participants over the longer term involves numerous difficulties, especially if they have left the institution through which they were recruited. Abortion rates are only one measure of unwanted pregnancies, and the study also looked at live births by age 20, but although rates were lower for the intervention group than for the control group, the difference was not statistically significant. The research team were able to show that peer-led sex education was more popular with pupils than conventional lessons on the topic delivered by teaching staff, but the follow-up survey conducted at age 18 showed that the use of contraception and the incidence of sexually transmitted infections were not significantly different between the intervention and control groups. This suggested that a relatively limited intervention of three one-hour peer-led sessions could not on its own solve the problem of teenagers taking risks in their sexual behaviour, although the study did suggest that its popularity among pupils meant that it merited inclusion in more extensive programmes of sex education in schools. Furthermore, the team's findings challenged various common-sense suppositions including the familiar one that sex education reduces the age at which young people engage in sexual activity. They used the findings additionally to propose broadening the curriculum to take it away from its overly biological focus, which Oakley's long-standing interest in the sex/gender distinction made her particularly well-placed to do.

The RIPPLE study was one of three social interventions using randomised controlled trials with which Oakley was involved that she and Vicki Strange, Tami Toroyan, Meg Wiggins, Ian Roberts and Judith Stephenson (a subset of the teams which worked on the three projects) reflected on in a 2003 publication to draw more general conclusions about research involving random allocation of participants. One of the other two projects built upon the social support and motherhood study through the investigation of social support and family health by comparing the results and cost effectiveness of two types of intervention supporting mothers and children in two disadvantaged boroughs in inner London. Cost effectiveness was also a consideration in the study of the provision of high-quality day care through a local authority Early Years Centre in a different inner London borough, indicating the importance of economic considerations to the process of evaluation, in this case looking at the impact of the service provision on maternal employment and income. In none of the projects was the random allocation of participants straightforward, but Oakley and her colleagues nevertheless concluded that efforts put into explaining the logic of the approach to participants and members of stakeholder organisations paid dividends in terms of participation rates and research results. They also drew on their experience of the three studies to identify useful lessons to share regarding good practice when incorporating randomisation in research design, for example, by including some tangible benefits for control groups that are more immediate than the long-term advancement of knowledge to which their participation contributes. In this way, Oakley and her colleagues rebutted the more practical objections raised by social scientists about the feasibility and ethicality of randomised controlled trials, although they acknowledged that such advice would not overcome the more deep-seated opposition of critics whose stance on research paradigm incommensurability led them to consider trials an inappropriate method for social science altogether. Oakley and her colleagues' article made the further important point that systematic reviews of existing research on the field being investigated would ideally have been undertaken prior to trials being conducted in order to inform thinking about the theoretical rationales for the interventions.

Oakley and her SSRU/EPPI Centre colleagues conducted numerous systematic reviews that revealed a tendency for researchers to over-claim when evaluating the success of their own research. This applied in health studies, education and criminology research and beyond. Objecting to having their professional judgement questioned on methodological grounds led some researchers to accuse Oakley and her colleagues of positivist bias; they in response rejected the idea that systematic reviewing treated quantitative studies as inherently superior to qualitative ones. Oakley viewed it as more constructive to leave paradigm wars behind and to treat quantitative and qualitative approaches as complementary rather than epistemologically incompatible. She was, moreover, keen to demonstrate the case that she was making rather than simply asserting it as a theoretical proposition. Examining the literature on teenage pregnancy and social disadvantage provided one such opportunity. Working with Angela Harden, Ginny Brunton and Adam Fletcher, Oakley sought to show the value of integrating quantitative and qualitative research by conducting a systematic review of 10 interventions involving controlled trials, a thematic synthesis of five qualitative studies of young people's experiences and, thirdly, an exercise integrating the two sets of findings. The logic of doing so was that qualitative data enhanced the interpretation of the quantitative data relating to statistical relationships such as those between growing up in materially disadvantaged circumstances, disengagement from schooling and having a child as a teenager. Systematically reviewing these interventions indicated that positive outcomes were associated with programmes aimed at preschool children and with those aimed at teenagers, but it took the integration of these statistical findings with the qualitative data to comprehend how material disadvantage and related unhappiness bred both low self-esteem and the limited expectations and aspirations that the young people (young men as well as young women) had for the future that could make early parenthood appear relatively attractive. Because all six interventions that were judged sound enough to have usable findings were American while the five qualitative studies were UK-based caution was required when integrating the two types of material. The team nevertheless concluded that sex education and the provision of sexual health services could not on their own produce the desired reduction in the United Kingdom's high rate of teenage pregnancy.

Oakley and her colleagues' analysis of teenage pregnancy and social disadvantage contributed to a growing literature on the subject which supported the case for policy interventions at different life stages. The systematic review of the trial results identified benefits of interventions in early childhood to enhance preschool education, while community work with teenagers also showed positive results, as did work with their parents to enhance their parenting skills from childbirth onwards. The opportunity also arose to identify topics that might usefully be the subject of future trials through discussion of issues that the qualitative material flagged up as relevant to young people's lived experience but which had not been fully explored quantitatively, such as bullying at school as a factor to which policymakers' attention should be drawn. Altogether, the qualitative data highlighted 18 issues as relevant to understanding how young people could become disenchanted with and disengaged from conventional teenage trajectories towards adulthood. Diagrammatic representation of these revealed the complex interconnections between young people's home, school and community environments and their perceived futures. A generation previously Chelly Halsey (Oakley's most inspirational undergraduate tutor) had developed similar arguments about the challenges facing policymakers in the 1960s. They sought to break cycles of poverty and deprivation into which children from disadvantaged families were born, became trapped, and were fated in turn as adults to pass on to their own children. The projects with which Halsey was associated used the language of intervention and experiment and were characterised by over-optimism regarding the benefits that social science could bring to solving social problems, a point that critics were quick to make when the results turned out to be less transformational than hoped. Halsey identified Richard Titmuss as a key influence on his thinking, not least because of his interest in the relative importance of heredity and social environment as determinants of a person's life chances. Oakley's early *Sex, Gender and Society* had likewise grappled with the relationship between biology and sociology, and by the 1990s, she was also immersing herself in the complexities of the task which both Titmuss and Halsey had dedicated themselves, harnessing social science for the public good.

The national political context in which Oakley developed her engagement with social policy issues differed greatly from that of the 1960s when Titmuss and Halsey collaborated with Harold Wilson's earlier Labour governments. Social scientists working during the 18 years of Conservative governments ushered in by Margaret Thatcher's 1979 general election victory faced a much less receptive audience for their ideas among policymakers. The compulsory renaming imposed on their principal funding body as the Economic and Social Research Council (ESRC) discouraged the notion that they were scientists and came with cuts to that organisation's budget. By the early 1980s, Oakley was already engaging with policymaking through her work with the World Health Organization. This led her to argue that the measurement of the outcome of childbirth should look beyond the predominant focus on death rates among infants and mothers to include the psychosocial considerations that her study of motherhood had identified as meriting greater attention. Her subsequent study of social support and pregnancy outcomes extended further the discussion of policy-related issues to include important matters like cigarette smoking among pregnant women. Oakley noted that despite extensive evidence of smoking's harmful effects on fetuses, health professionals exhorting mothers to give it up was on its own unlikely to be effective. This was because of the way that women in stressful situations used smoking as a means of coping; in consequence, ameliorating the stresses they faced (for example, through providing social support) was a surer route to cessation, as other feminist researchers had also argued. Hilary Graham's identification of smoking as a coping strategy used by lone mothers was borne out by Oakley's finding that smoking rates were highest among women not living with their baby's father. These were a minority of the mothers in *Social Support and Motherhood*, but the fact that 69% of them were smokers (compared to 40% of the sample overall) was nevertheless telling. The statistically significant association of lower rates of smoking with higher household incomes and with owner-occupied housing provided indications of how people's material situations can influence their health outcomes, markedly so when social inequalities widen as rapidly as they did in the 1980s.

An early SSRU initiative saw Oakley organise a seminar series focusing on health, education and welfare. Discussions about recent policy changes constituting a threat to (even the dismantling of) the welfare state provided the backdrop. Along with her SSRU colleague A. Susan Williams, Oakley co-edited the written versions of the seminar presentations in book form, published in 1994 as *The Politics of the Welfare State*. Her introduction to the wide-ranging collection reflected on the origins and development of the welfare state as well as key contemporary challenges. She identified the 1970s as a watershed decade in which the long-term trend towards reducing social inequalities went into reverse and a new paradigm for analysing welfare emerged. Oakley gave due credit to Titmuss's writings which had epitomised the Fabian approach to welfare associated with the London School of Economics, promoting progress towards the new type of society envisaged by the architects of the fundamental reforms to education, health, social security, housing and social planning more generally dating from the 1940s. In addition, however, she noted that prioritising the goal of ameliorating social class inequalities appeared rather out of touch to activists involved in identity politics who were challenging injustices in relation to other dimensions of social inequality. In particular the women's and gay liberation movements and parallel efforts concerned with race and ethnicity, disability and ageing were celebrating diversity, asserting pride against experienced prejudice and demanding a greater say in the organisation and delivery of welfare services. The slogan 'nothing about us without us' captured this. Such sentiments fitted Oakley's own experience of paternalistic treatment at the hands of medical professionals and chimed with broader concerns that women and various 'minority' groups had the status of second-class citizens when outcomes were compared. Disadvantaged citizens asserting their entitlement to the same standard of welfare as everyone else were, however, out of sync with policymaking in the 1980s as it moved away from uniform provision in education, health and welfare provision and towards the facilitation of choice that came with market-based reforms in public services. As new patterns of social inequality emerged, continued scrutiny of rhetoric and reality was needed.

The changing socio-economic context of welfare provision was also the focus of a wide-ranging research initiative on the management of personal welfare which Oakley co-ordinated with Jennie Popay, funded from 1990 to 1995 jointly by the ESRC and the Joseph Rowntree Foundation. Gender was a core concern in this initiative, building on feminists' efforts to highlight women's welfare and the contribution made by women to the welfare of others, not least the unpaid caring work carried out within families which frequently went unacknowledged (or at least uncounted). Much of the research undertaken to reorient this field had been qualitative, prompting reconsideration of social policy's underpinning research methods. This reassessment included growing appreciation of comparative research, which revealed the UK welfare state's unusual profile and consequently its limited usefulness as a standard point of reference. Also of methodological significance were innovations in the evaluation of policy initiatives associated with the development of systematic reviewing through the Cochrane Collaboration with its philosophy of using randomised controlled trials to reduce bias when deciding whether health interventions should be deemed effective. These rationales for reflecting on research methods were closely aligned with Oakley's experience of using a randomised controlled trial in the social support and pregnancy outcomes study and her broader concern with mixing methods. Oakley, Popay and Fiona Williams discussed this in the introductory chapter to their 1999 co-edited collection *Welfare Research: A Critical Review* that arose from the initiative. In addition, the book allowed Oakley to revisit the contrast between health professionals' and mothers' perspectives on reproduction about which she and Hilary Graham had written in 1981, for which Oakley had drawn on data from the becoming a mother study. Contrasting that account with findings from more recent studies (including *Social Support and Motherhood*) she and her co-authors Jeanette Edwards and Popay observed that the shift towards more female health professionals that had occurred in the intervening period had been insufficient to close the gap that existed between service providers' and users' perspectives on welfare needs. Female users' understandings drawn from their immediate lived experience continued to be in tension with the training that service providers received and the institutional constraints within which they had to operate.

Oakley's longstanding argument that research on gender should not be treated as synonymous with the study of women's lives informed several parts of the initiative's investigations into the management of personal welfare. The title chosen by Popay, Edwards and Jeff Hearn as co-editors of the 1998 collection that arose from the initiative, *Men, Gender Divisions and Welfare*, highlighted the importance of the point. The relational nature of gender and masculinity's role in its reproduction came through particularly starkly in discussions of men's violence against women, including that occurring within domestic settings. In her contribution to this collection, Oakley and her co-author Alan Rigby treated violence (including the threat of violence) against women as a neglected public health issue, noting its part in the story of how men and women experience families differently. Gendered identities shape how men and women make different contributions to families and derive different benefits and harms from being part of them. For example, the caring responsibilities allocated to women have positive conse-quences for the mental health of other family members but can work to the detriment of their own. Oakley's analysis of postnatal depression captured in microcosm how the alloca-tion to women of responsibility for others' personal welfare makes family relationships stressful. Oakley and Rigby did not claim to be the first to have developed this line of argu-ment, acknowledging that the case for scrutinising the work-ings of the family through a focus on the unequal positions of women and men had been made long before. The pioneering research into women's dependence that Eleanor Rathbone conducted earlier in the 20th century stood out in their view because she had revealed the error of assuming that a husband earning a 'family wage' sufficient to meet the needs of his wife and children as well as himself would allocate his income accordingly. Of course, the introduction of various welfare provisions (such as family allowances paid to mothers) and the growth of married women's employment meant that wives' dependence on male breadwinners became less marked than it had been in Rathbone's day, but it was nevertheless clear that the welfare state had not fully resolved this problem.

Historical contextualisation has always characterised Oakley's work, from her early studies of housework and of motherhood to her 2024 book *The Science of Housework* tracing the fluctuating fortunes of domestic science as an academic discipline. Her engagement with issues of personal welfare and the welfare state also drew her towards historical comparisons, including through critical reconsideration of her late father's canonical writings. The early argument that Titmuss put forward with his wife Kay in their wartime book *Parents Revolt* was of interest because it projected a declining birth rate; although erroneous, it nevertheless invited attention for the reasoning by which they reached this conclusion. The influence on Titmuss's thinking of the Eugenics Society was the subject of a 1991 article, expanded on by Oakley in *Man and Wife*. Titmuss's emphasis on the impact of people's social and economic circumstances on their health placed him at odds with those Eugenics Society members who accorded greater weight to the influence of biological inheritance on population profiles, but it also facilitated dialogue with others who shared his view about environmental factors. Rathbone was among this group, renowned for championing the cause of widows and other impoverished mothers in her campaigns for welfare reform. The attention that Rathbone drew to differences in available domestic budgets was revisited in debates among feminists of Oakley's generation about what women had in common and what separated them (for example, in relation to the distinctive position of lone mothers). The brief history of gender that Oakley contributed to *Who's Afraid of Feminism?* was one place where she reflected on women's welfare within different household types. She also grappled there with another long-standing debate to which her father had contributed and which resurfaced as part of the backlash against second wave feminism, that of the relationship between biological and social influences on the making of women and men (and other categorisations of people beyond gendered ones). Further consideration was given to how far eugenic thinking had come in the age of sociobiology and evolutionary psychology in Oakley's *Essays on Women, Medicine and Health* and in *Gender on Planet Earth* where she discussed the dystopian portrayal of the politics of reproduction in literature such as Margaret Atwood's novel *The Handmaid's Tale* to which Charlotte Perkins Gilman's more optimistic fictional vision *Herland* from a century previously could be contrasted.

Oakley did not share completely Titmuss's critique of what he called the irresponsible society, but sufficient overlap existed among the social ills they identified for the term to appear in her own writing. Their shared view that powerful positions come with responsibilities to less privileged citizens led them both to bemoan medical professionals' high-handedness towards patients and to decry the limited accountability of politicians to their electorate (the majority of whom, Titmuss noted, were women). The durability of Titmuss's writings prompted Oakley to work with others on their republication together with commentaries that explored their contemporary relevance. His final book *The Gift Relationship* championed altruism over transactional relationships, using blood donation to illustrate his analysis of individual and collective welfare. At a time when market-based reforms were being extended in various policy areas, including health, the book's republication in 1997 provided a timely reminder of how the common good can be enhanced by individual citizens voluntarily contributing to the welfare of strangers via a collective arrangement, the National Blood Transfusion Service. Oakley was more concerned than Titmuss about the gendered distribution of expected altruism which she argued reflected women being associated with service and care work (both unpaid care in families and the professional responsibilities of nurses); this could result in their feeling bad about themselves despite doing good, she argued. Nevertheless, sufficient examples of altruism provided hope that the idealised figure of rational economic man she had first encountered as an undergraduate had not swept all before him. Another example of altruism emerged from studies of people's motivations for taking part in medical research, where participants' desire to help others through assisting in the advancement of knowledge to everyone's potential benefit sat alongside possible gains to themselves through the treatment that they received. Like Titmuss's research on altruism, Oakley noted, these studies were produced by a combination of quantitative and qualitative methods, thereby epitomising the challenge that she set herself in writing *Experiments in Knowing*, to determine how we have arrived at our current state of knowledge. Gender featured prominently in explaining how different ways of knowing have emerged, and sometimes (like the informally derived knowledge of early midwives) been eclipsed.

Knowledge is not straightforwardly cumulative, as the history of science shows. Oakley's relationship to Titmuss's work exemplifies how no generation of researchers builds on predecessors' work in a simple additive fashion. Over time, research questions change as shifts occur in conceptual frameworks, as methodological practice develops and as agendas evolve, periodically involving dramatic reorientation. Feminism's impact on sociological thinking in the 1970s to which Oakley contributed demanded reconsideration of these fundamental issues of what should be researched, how it should be researched and why. One emergent idea was that women's marginal position in society generates distinctive ways of knowing and that qualitative methods are the route to accessing these, but while Oakley accepted much of the critique of malestream social scientific knowledge on which this argument rested, she rejected putting to one side the use of quantitative methods and the notion of scientific enquiry. Her experience of confronting biases and other shortcomings in malestream thinking provided Oakley with a springboard for her work in evaluation and systematic reviewing which revealed alarming biases in academic endeavour generally, malestream and otherwise. Oakley found it problematic, for example, that Mary Belenky and her colleagues' influential 1986 study *Women's Ways of Knowing* rested on an all-female sample, since their argument was framed in terms of what was distinctive about women's experiences compared to men's, but their knowledge of the latter was second-hand and not directly comparable. In addition, by adding an interview question during their fieldwork, these researchers raised suspicion that they were too keen to find what they were looking for. Oakley's general position was that the choice of methods should always be appropriate to the research problem being investigated, and sometimes this means using randomised controlled trials. This is applied in medical research into breast cancer where striking advances in knowledge about effective treatments had occurred, directly benefitting the one in 12 UK women who develop that condition. Research into other medical conditions conversely revealed the dangers of over-treatment and excessive medicalisation. What Oakley termed practical feminism took as its goal knowledge that minimises bias and can be shown to be helpful to women in their everyday lives.

Oakley's own research reminded her of the need for vigilance concerning bias. In the social support and pregnancy outcomes study, it became apparent that what was known about the extent of smoking among pregnant women depended on how questions were asked. In a self-administered questionnaire, the prospective mothers who smoked gave an average figure of 16.6 cigarettes consumed per day, over 25% higher than the figure of 13 given to research midwives in face-to-face interviews; the apparent underreporting to the latter suggests women's sensitivity to health professionals' known disapproval of smoking. Comparing research findings collected at different times presents further questions about the status of the knowledge generated, as Oakley and her SSRU

colleagues Meg Wiggins, Vicki Strange, Mary Sawtell and
Helen Austerberry appreciated when conducting a repeat study
of the becoming a mother project. More than 30 years separated the two projects, and although efforts were made to
ensure their similarity while investigating continuity and
change in the experience of becoming a mother, a precise
replication was neither possible nor desirable. Recruitment
through the research hospital in west London was among
features of the two studies that stayed the same, and the
research methods used in both projects were similar, as were
the numbers of mothers who participated, 58 in the second
compared to 55 in the first. But the source of the research
funding changed (ESRC for the first, the British United Prov-
ident Association or the BUPA Foundation for the second), and
the participants in the 2000s were markedly more diverse than
their 1970s counterparts as recruitment criteria were relaxed,
resulting in the inclusion of women from non-white ethnic
backgrounds and women who had a same-sex partner, who
lived apart from their partner or who had no partner (although
white women living with heterosexual partners still constituted
the majority). Social changes in the intervening period were
reflected in the mothers' average age being 26 in the first study
and 31 in the second, and these latter participants having a
higher social class profile. These differences, along with policy
shifts towards care being more woman-centred than it had
been in the 1970s, all qualified statements that could be made
about broad patterns of change.

Policy changes affected the experience of new motherhood
for the women in the second study, notwithstanding the
methodological caveats about the two projects' differences.
Paid paternity leave had not been available in the 1970s, and
although not all partners of the second study's mothers took
the full two weeks entitlement, the majority did, and some
took unpaid leave in addition. Their presence at home may

have contributed to the average length of the women's stay in
hospital being only 2.4 days, less than the 9 days of the first
study when partners returned to work shortly after their
child's birth, and considerably shorter than Kay Titmuss's 13-
day hospital stay when having Ann. The second study also
found changed norms around a partner's presence at the birth;
in the 21st century, it has become the expectation, in contrast
to when the agreement of medical staff had been necessary for
husbands to be present. The researchers wanted to know how
much the balance of power between mothers and medical staff
had shifted. The expectation that prospective mothers would
be better informed (not least because of the information and
social support available through the internet) suggested that
Oakley's critique of medicalisation might require revision, in
particular regarding the experience of technological interventions as alienating and medical professionals overriding
women's wishes. In fact, the second study's findings were
mixed; a higher proportion of the mothers reported having
good levels of control over the process, but sizeable minorities
expressed dissatisfaction with the care that they received from
health professionals including that from doctors, midwives
and health visitors. Medical interventions remained prominent: of the 58 mothers, 25 (43%) had caesarean sections. At
the other end of the spectrum running from medicalised to
natural childbirth, there were 11 vaginal births without
induced labours, epidurals or other intervention; most of these
took place in the hospital's midwife-led birthing centre. The
researchers' expectation that the second study's participants
would report less shock in relation to the process of becoming
a mother was not universally borne out. Having more information, more support (including from private service providers such as doulas in addition to that from partners) and
more choice (compared to their 1970s counterparts) did not

necessarily make the mothers' experience a comfortable one, either practically or emotionally.

A systematic review of 60 studies of first-time mothers in the United Kingdom that Oakley conducted with Wiggins and Ginny Brunton broadly confirmed the repeat study's main themes, including the finding that women's views about the quality of the care that they received had not changed markedly from those of 30 years previously. There was little evidence that various initiatives, including Oakley's promotion of improved social support, had facilitated women becoming mothers more on their own terms than according to others' templates. Oakley also sought further perspectives on the becoming a mother study by re-interviewing those original participants who could be traced nearly 40 years on, who were by then in their later fifties or sixties. Of the original 55, some had died, some were uncontactable and some declined to participate, but 36 (65%) were re-interviewed either by Oakley (who conducted 17 interviews) or by another research team member (Austerberry, Sawtell or Wiggins). A question was included about whether being repeatedly interviewed by a sociologist as they became first-time mothers had influenced them. Typical answers were positive enough, framed in terms of finding it interesting to reflect on their experiences, with the possibility of other women being helped by their involvement. Nevertheless, a full third of the mothers re-interviewed had very little if any recollection of taking part, including one of the women whose child's birth Oakley had attended. Another woman remembered the original interviews including questions about women's liberation that she had found skewed, while a few others had been in two minds whether to accept the invitation to be re-interviewed because talking about their lives would take them back to difficult past experiences which they preferred to leave behind. For most, they recalled being happy enough to share their thoughts with Oakley in the

1970s without the interviews constituting life-changing events, and after the final interview, they had simply moved on, in at least one case sceptical of the potential of research to change policy. The project thus provided a reminder of how memory is selective, as Oakley was also discovering through studies of previous generations of women social scientists to which her attention was increasingly gravitating.

6

HISTORICAL BIOGRAPHICAL RESEARCH

Oakley's early critique of sociologists' obeisance towards the discipline's founding fathers implied a corresponding neglect of, even disregard for, the history of women social scientists. Much later, after handing over the Social Science Research Unit Director's role, she was able to address this intellectual sexism properly. She did so using various formats which began with *A Critical Woman*, her full-length biography of Barbara Wootton, proceeded through consideration of the ideas and campaigning of 328 first wave feminists in *Women, Peace and Welfare* and then produced a third book, *Forgotten Wives*, about four individuals whose marriages to famous men fated them to be overshadowed, and a fourth, *The Science of Housework*, on women who strove to establish the academic credentials of domestic science. In these projects, Oakley had to contend with the challenges of working with diverse archival material relating to people no longer alive, many of whom in their lifetimes had been subject to misrepresentation and lambasted as difficult women. Her parents and her father's institutional base (the London School of Economics, or LSE) provided connections to several of them, including

childhood memories of visiting Wootton in the Surrey coun-
tryside and of the economic historian and theorist of equality
R H Tawney (the husband of one of the forgotten wives)
visiting her Acton house. Oakley was already familiar with the
challenges of constructing biographical accounts using
archival material through writing a short piece about Millicent Fawcett along with the book about her parents' early life
together, *Man and Wife*, that emerged from scrutinising the
contents of the suitcase her mother left her and from the
responsibilities of succeeding her mother as her father's literary executor. Oakley also endeavoured in *Father and
Daughter* to understand better insufficiently appreciated
women when considering her father's female social work
colleagues with whom he frequently clashed. Several things
contribute to women being hidden from history (to use Sheila
Rowbotham's celebrated phrase). This may happen by women
being accorded lower status and consequently less attention
and respect than men, by active suppression of records of their
achievements or by their being overlooked and forgotten
about. Appropriate remembering helps to prevent knowledge
being skewed by gender-biased selectivity that at best locates
women in the background and at worst makes them invisible.
More positively, it promotes fairer representations of how
contemporary societies and academic disciplines have come
about.

Photographs figure in all five of these books in which
Oakley sought to counteract the forces that, by making men
the centre of attention, relegate women to the sidelines. They
do not necessarily relay unbiased, unambiguous truths about
social relationships better than other archival sources, but
they do prompt curiosity. Why, for example, was Ellen
Swallow Richards the sole woman alongside 25 men in the
1900 photograph of Massachusetts Institute of Technology
chemistry staff? And why was Wootton the only female

among recipients of honorary degrees at various UK universities in the 1960s and 1970s (one more than in the all-male
group of honorary degree recipients at another university
which included Richard Titmuss)? In another time and place,
it was Titmuss who was marginal in a photograph that
captured his wife Kay alongside the royal visitor to the centre
for unemployed people in interwar London where she
worked. At that point, the new husband was still learning
about the presentation of self from his wife who had had a
superior education and more cultured upbringing. *Man and
Wife* tells the story of a future professor being moulded, with
Kay's contribution to his academic success coming at the cost
of her own withdrawal from the public sphere in order to fulfil
the role of helpmate wife (known alternatively by the economist J K Galbraith's term servant-wife). Photographic records
created for public consumption can be illuminating without
necessarily capturing the personal troubles and how they are
privately experienced to which Charles Wright Mills referred
in the quotation used to open *Man and Wife*. The book relies
heavily on correspondence, diaries and other personal documents to convey how her parents' lives did not always tally
with the myths told about them, including the myth (which
Kay promulgated) of Richard's saintliness. The shaping and
enhancement of reputations is a craft that requires an eye for
what materials to preserve and what to withhold from future
archival researchers. Oakley was mindful of her mother's
careful pruning of the suitcase's contents, leaving the same
questions about missing data as are raised by reports of people
consigning papers to bonfires or shredders to keep personal or
family information secret. She later discovered Wootton was
another destroyer of such materials.

Man and Wife is revealing about how, with Kay's seemingly
inexhaustible support and encouragement, Richard Titmuss
succeeded in making a name for himself despite relatively

humble beginnings. One way of getting noticed was by nuisance behaviour, writing to the Registrar General and others in positions of authority pestering them for population statistics (for example) in a manner akin to freedom of information requests lodged today. Another was writing extensively (occasionally jointly with Kay) in various formats and being undeterred by publishers' rejections when submitting these letters, articles and books for publication. The independent mindedness of these writings suggested that not having a university degree left him free from intellectual straitjackets and allowed him to think imaginatively. A third means of raising his profile was the cultivation of connections with like-minded people who appreciated his line of thought about the health of the nation, notably the detailed evidential approach that underpinned his argument about fertility rates. Joining the Eugenics Society in 1937 proved particularly fruitful in this regard as it provided access to a circle of influential figures in academia and policymaking. His expanding network exercised a magnetic pull towards the LSE where many of the society's members worked or had close links. Oakley's 1991 article in the *British Journal of Sociology* described her father's developing engagement at the level of ideas with this network which helped to pave the way for his appointment as an LSE professor in 1950, but more archival work was needed before the fuller story of informal as well as formal interactions could be told in *Man and Wife*, published in 1996, nearly a decade after the suitcase came into her possession. Personal correspondence between her father and Jerry Morris betrayed his vulnerability to imposter syndrome when in the company of better-educated people; fortunately for their remarkable later collaboration on social medicine, his friend gave this lack of confidence short shrift. Further letters revealed that Morris was equally dependent on his helpmate wife, Galia. Kay's diary of her wartime pregnancy also featured Galia providing practical support as Kay's apprehension rose about her approaching due date, while Richard's demands on her secretarial skills continued unabated.

Man and Wife was not the only book of Oakley's that she encountered difficulties writing. The patchiness of the historical material from which pregnancy and childbirth from women's viewpoint could be gleaned is lamented in *The Captured Womb*, for example, while the converse problem of having more data than can easily be managed is noted in *Women Confined*. When discussing her parents' lives, a key challenge related to the subject matter's literal closeness to home. Having castigated sociology's founding fathers for their exploitative and oppressive treatment of their wives, the conundrum of this scenario resembling her parents' marriage arose. Her mother's acquiescence to putting her husband's career first may have conformed to the norms of the time, but it was not inevitable. The Titmusses knew couples with children where both parents continued their professional work, including LSE colleagues David and Ruth Glass and the Swedish social scientists Gunnar and Alva Myrdal. The latter notably wrote about the impact of motherhood on women's careers which Oakley herself had to confront. Richard Titmuss's writings were less progressive than the Myrdals' about what his daughter would later call gender inequalities, partly because he paid less attention to the respective positions of men and women than he did to social class inequalities. Had he lived longer, he may well have been as shocked as his wife was about the ideas that their daughter put into the public domain criticising conventional models of family life as outmoded. Working on *Man and Wife* was also complicated by the poignancy associated with photographs of her father's unhealthy relationship with cigarettes that would eventually lead to his early death. The book was published shortly after *Young People, Health and Family Life* in which Oakley and her co-authors discussed young people's risk-taking; by this time, smoking had become a high-profile public health issue unlike in her father's youth, but public information campaigns still faced obstacles trying to change behaviour associated with seriously adverse effects likely to occur only some way into the future. Poignancy of a different sort was associated with letters that revealed her mother's ambition, ultimately unfulfilled, of writing a novel.

Man and Wife had a lengthy gestation period, as did *A Critical Woman*. Oakley read Wootton's work as an under-graduate and drew on her writings in *The Sociology of Housework, Subject Women, Social Support and Mother-hood, Man and Wife, Gender on Planet Earth* and elsewhere long before embarking on her biography. Born in 1897, Wootton was nearly 50 years Oakley's senior, but the two had much in common including academic parents, marriage at the age of 20 while still a student, intolerance of complacency about social matters and preparedness to contest rules that treated women less favourably than men (although Wootton did acquiesce to antiquated regulations requiring her lectures in economics delivered in 1920s Cambridge to be advertised under a man's name). Both contributed regularly to *New Society*. Another connection was their shared affiliation with Bedford College, where Wootton practised her philosophy that sociological research should be of practical use, devel-oped through evidence-based argument and avoid overly grandiose theorisation, anticipating much of Oakley's own vision. When the time came for promotion to professorial positions, neither chose to be known simply as a sociologist, although Wootton's time as Professor of Social Studies was marked by such hostility within the University of London that it led ultimately to her resignation. Her frustration with opponents to her ambitious plans for sociology at Bedford College was aired publicly through 'Reflections on Resigning a Professorship'. This predated by nearly two decades Oakley's registration as a Bedford College PhD student in 1969, but many of Wootton's complaints about research being stifled by academia's bureaucratic hierarchies became familiar to Professor Oakley, as her 1999 novel *Overheads* made clear. Prior to her own promotion, Oakley's poems in *Telling the Truth about Jerusalem* saw her wondering whether achieving professorial status would be worth the personal cost, in her case the risk of attenuating her relationship with her children. Wootton was married twice but had no children, and this difference between her and Oakley (for whom having children was pivotal to the development of her feminism) may offer a clue as to why Wootton did not identify as a feminist.

As Wootton's biographer, Oakley recognised the dangers of over-identification with her subject. The title of Wootton's autobiography, *In a World I Never Made*, used the line from A E Housman's poem to convey her sense of being a stranger and the book detailed her own and other women's experiences of being treated as an outgroup in a man's world. Wootton's acute awareness of women's second-class status did not lead her to adopt a feminist stance, however, and her antipathy towards feminism and feminists remained puzzling for Oakley. Timing may have been part of the explanation, as much of Wootton's work was done between the periods of intellectual ferment and activism that marked feminism's first and second waves. Also possibly at play was her temperament, often identified as iconoclastic, sometimes more straightforwardly described as lacking warmth towards others beyond her circle of friends. This characteristic suggests a reason for Wootton's life and career disappearing from mainstream consciousness within a few years of her death in 1988. Wootton was an agnostic and cared little about how she might be remembered. Unlike her contemporary Richard Titmuss, she did not build connections with people who might have preserved her reputation as a formidable social critic and reformer. A fellow academic who knew them both regarded Titmuss as a less brilliant social analyst, hinting that enduring fame may also reflect human qualities such as approachability. Oakley, however, suspected that gendered assumptions about supposedly difficult people contributed to Wootton's public reputation. Thirty interviews conducted with individuals who had known her allowed Oakley to gain a more rounded sense of her personality. Oakley may still not have warmed to Wootton but admired her determination and rigour as a social scientist which made her something of a heroine. Bowlby's work on maternal deprivation that had been discussed in Oakley's first publication was subjected in Wootton's *Social Science and Social Pathology* to formidable dissection on methodological, theoretical and conceptual grounds. Nor was Wootton's scepticism about the idea that delinquency might be attributed to shortcomings in the relationships that adolescents had with their mothers purely academic; Wootton was a magistrate in the juvenile courts for 44 years, in that time dealing with the sentencing of over 8,000 young people. Her second husband, George Wright, had himself been part of an earlier cohort of juvenile delinquents, Wootton once revealed.

Wootton's remarkable breadth of interests was coupled with disregard for disciplinary boundaries; combined with an acerbic writing style, this led to academic swords being crossed. Social workers took particular exception to her critique of their claims that their discipline embodied scientific expertise relating to antisocial behaviour for which she found no grounds in her thorough examination of the literature. Oakley could draw parallels to her own challenge to medical expertise and to her championing of systematic reviewing as a way of discovering the state of the knowledge base in a particular field. She also found Wootton's critique of the concept of problem families ahead of its time, querying the phenomenon of married women undertaking paid work being treated as a concerning deviation from the ideal household headed by a male breadwinner with women confined to domestic duties. Economists were another disciplinary group that Wootton took to task. Her 1938 book *Lament for Economics* bemoaned neoclassical economic teachings that were presented in a way that is unintelligible to ordinary people, that ignored reality and that were of no practical use; Oakley echoed these sentiments decades later. Economists' refusal to engage with Wootton's ideas consigned her to the group of women writers on economics marginalised by historians of the discipline; that group included Clara Elizabeth Collet, Charlotte Perkins Gilman and Rosa Luxemburg, all of whom featured in *Women, Peace and Welfare*. Oakley's critique of rational economic man was aligned with Wootton's research regarding the unequal levels of reward paid to different groups of workers. Wootton's examination of the factors determining the relative salaries of teachers, civil servants, nurses and prison officers had as a logical extension Oakley's concern with housework being unpaid. Wootton's useful capacity to reframe the way questions were posed about diverse issues continued after 1958, when she became the first woman life peer. By participating in the work of the House of Lords, she exercised a direct influence on policymaking, and she used this platform to influence debates on laws relating to marriage, abortion, capital punishment, drugs, road safety and numerous other topics in the course of 1,792 speeches.

At various points, Wootton touched on the concept of motivation and revealed its importance well beyond psychology. Her critique of neoclassical economics included scepticism about explanations of behaviour framed in terms of economic rationality where the motive of profit maximisation rules (people may be motivated by altruism, for example), while her criminological writing challenged the legal view that what mattered when determining punishment was an offender's intention. Oakley felt that Wootton's analyses would have benefitted from greater engagement with American social science such as Mills's work on vocabularies of motive. Wootton's own motivations were naturally of interest to her biographer in seeking to understand what drove her. Oakley noted that Wootton's thinking was characterised by morality rooted not in formal religion but in her socialist and humanist convictions: some things, such as social inequality and nuclear weapons, were simply wrong. Oakley dedicated the biography to Vera Seal who had supported Wootton in various capacities for over half of her life. Seal's contribution to the book was pivotal, not least for the insight that Wootton's apparent standoffishness masked an underlying shyness and insecurity. The steady supply of information and observations sent to Oakley, sometimes daily, made her the project's key informant. In her efforts to understand her subject, Oakley travelled to places important to Wootton and observed that she was drawn from midlife onwards to rural life, as was true also for Oakley. Reflections about their many academic and personal points of connection raised for her the question of whether another biographer might have produced an account of Wootton's life and work that diverged from hers in significant respects. She was aware nevertheless that the overlaps between their two lives made her particularly well-suited to the role and to see it through despite the scale of the task expanding significantly beyond that initially envisaged. One of the aspects of her own life that came into clearer view through the study of Wootton's was the role of serendipity in opening new directions of travel rather than paths forward being consciously planned, and their accounts of their lives in this respect are far from unusual.

Wootton's discussion of serendipity in her autobiography acknowledged forerunners who refused to accept the world as it was and strove to improve opportunities for future generations, including the right of women to vote. A principal figure in the suffrage movement, Millicent Fawcett, had been the subject of Oakley's first venture into archive-based bio-graphical writing in the early 1980s. Although Oakley's chapter was considerably shorter than the Wootton biogra-phy, a week in the archives was sufficient to reveal the more complicated reality behind the public face that Fawcett pre-sented. Oakley had been commissioned to write the chapter for a book on feminist theorists, and a key issue requiring explanation was Fawcett's disagreements not only with many men but also a good number of women. Her objections to the more militant wing of the movement for women's suffrage were partly about political strategy and tactics, but they were also about political values since her radicalism in pursuit of women's right to vote was combined with more conservative attitudes towards family life and individual responsibility than those held by campaigners such as Eleanor Rathbone; cam-paigning for the extension of the franchise did not make Fawcett a revolutionary. Learning more about her personal life (including her childhood) allowed Oakley to locate Faw-cett's feminism alongside her commitment to other causes including her support for nationalism that so divided opinions during the First World War. Oakley would return in *Women, Peace and Welfare* to Fawcett's critics who aligned themselves to an international peace movement. The more rounded understanding of Fawcett that Oakley gained from archival research included some amusing anecdotal material, including her career as a novelist that saw a promising start with a story containing strongly autobiographical elements followed by failure of a second novel published pseudonymously in order to discover if the initial success was down to the author's fame rather than the quality of the writing. Oakley did not find that learning more about her made her subject more likeable, but she did draw the conclusion that accounts of lives presented in public should be treated with caution, and that it is always worthwhile excavating other sides of any story.

After *A Critical Woman*, Oakley's next book was *Father and Daughter*. This also revisited established accounts of people's lives, principally that of her father but those of people around him as well. The latter included the female social work colleagues in his LSE department with whom he protractedly had difficult relations. This story was uniquely challenging to excavate because Oakley recalled it (or at least her father's version of it) from childhood, when its latest instalments were related to her mother and her in detail at evening mealtimes. By the time she came to research what was known as 'the LSE affair', Oakley's decades of university experience had prepared her for competing narratives of academic contention. Indeed, not being appointed to the directorship of the Thomas Coram Research Unit gave her first-hand knowledge of the impact that appointing an outsider to a leadership position can have on established staff, especially where issues of gender politics and qualifications for the job are involved. In Titmuss's case, the issue of qualifications concerned both his lack of formal educational credentials and his limited knowledge of social work beyond that gleaned from his wife Kay, herself unqualified. The fact that the LSE social work staff for whom Richard Titmuss was given management responsibility in the newly independent Department of Social Administration had a history of being paid less than lecturers deemed active in research and were mainly female added to the tensions, as did his appointment of young men like Brian Abel-Smith, Peter Townsend and David Donnison who shared his research interests, while talented older women such as Pearl Jephcott were not retained. Oakley noted in his defence that her father had been insufficiently apprised by those who appointed him of the distinguished history of LSE social workers, including some still in post when he arrived. But any unwitting slights to which this lack of appreciation led were insignificant compared to his handling, or mishandling, of the reorgan- isation of social work training at the LSE for which Eileen Younghusband had secured prestigious funding from the Carnegie Trust. Oakley's analysis of the episode highlighted how gendered conflicts can be interwoven in complicated ways with social class distinctions and disciplinary affiliations.

Unearthing the story of what followed her father's appointment at the LSE brought several unwelcome surprises for Oakley. One was a fuller appreciation of her father's fallibility. She knew that his saint-like portrayal was mythical, but the discovery of how he sought to take credit for Younghusband's Carnegie grant was nevertheless unsettling. Just as dismaying was his failure to support Younghusband's application for a readership despite her impressive achieve- ments at LSE over many years. This smacked of the gendered assumptions associated with the glass ceiling phenomenon, the routine denial of recognition and appropriate opportu- nities to women. Misogyny also lurked in the implied char- acterisation of Younghusband as hysterical, although Titmuss himself had been maligned through his critics' deployment of the categories of psychoanalysis. It would indeed have been saintly to turn the other cheek having been identified as not only incompetent and Machiavellian but also as pathological, psychopathic, infantile, neurotic and schizophrenic. One of Younghusband's supporters also opined (based on a brief encounter) that the latter term might apply also to Titmuss's thirteen-year-old daughter. Oakley was alarmed to discover this in an archived letter more than fifty years on. This use of such language to denigrate opponents suggests that Wootton's detection of a pseudo-scientific base to social work at that time held water. Titmuss endorsed Wootton's assessment, and rival disciplinary perspectives clearly contributed to the con- flict becoming entrenched. Another active fault line was the fact that Titmuss's opponents came from more privileged social class backgrounds than he and many of his supporters did. Alongside this was the gendered nature of the participants' wider professional and personal connections. Titmuss was no stranger to the importance of networks (the LSE Director at the time of Titmuss's appointment was someone with whom he had been connected for a decade through the Eugenics Society, for example), but he was unprepared for his opponents' mobilisation of what they called their 'girls' network' which had an international reach. Only some of the female social workers in the LSE department that Titmuss headed sided against him, however. Oakley found in this another disappointment, patriarchy's enduring capacity to pit women against each other.

Immersion in the LSE and other archives reinforced Oakley's sense that women get labelled as difficult when their assertion of autonomy, determination and strength makes men uncomfortable. They are challenging because of their independence from, rather than reliance on, male support. The perceived threat is particularly noticeable when women act not as individuals but collectively, as the mobilisation of the network of female social workers illustrated. Moreover, Oakley's archival research revealed that Titmuss's confrontation with the 'difficult' women of the LSE in the 1950s was merely a fraction of a much larger history in which women's solidarity had been an invaluable asset. That episode provided, serendipitously, a portal into the period 1880–1920, decades commonly regarded as the peak of first wave feminism. Oakley argued in *Women, Peace and Welfare* that these decades are wrongly equated with the struggle to gain the vote for women. Paying disproportionate attention to the suffrage issue caused the relative neglect of other campaigns, including efforts to pursue social reform and the promotion of welfare, the reduction of gender inequalities in the labour market, pacificism on the international stage and, in the domestic realm, progressive reconfiguration of family life and housework. Oakley included her younger self among those who, keen to challenge the world as they found it, may not always have appreciated the full significance of pioneering predecessors. Charlotte Perkins Gilman provides a good example. Gilman's critique of the position of housewives was noted by Oakley in *Housewife* and in *Subject Women* where her thoughts on girls' education and on motherhood also featured. Gilman's ideas also provided inspiration for three pieces of writing included in *Telling the Truth about Jerusalem* but it was not until later, in *Gender on Planet Earth* and then in *Women, Peace and Welfare*, that Oakley discussed these ideas in depth. More than 80 years Gilman's junior, Oakley nevertheless recognised many similarities between them. These included resisting the medicalised diagnosis of postnatal depression, determination to promote public discussion of housework's negative aspects, enthusiasm for sociology's capacity to highlight the interconnection of public and private issues, awareness of how novels can capture the contradictoriness of women's social position, and appreciation of imaginative contemplation on alternative social arrangements (for example, Gilman's advocacy of the kitchenless home).

Gilman's literary writings were integral to her work, criticising existing arrangements and exploring alternatives. Through fiction, Gilman contested the idea that isolation could solve the mental health issues of new mothers and imagined what a society populated solely by women and girls might look like, including what observations of such a world a male sociologist who came across it (including its vegetarianism) might make. Alongside fiction, Gilman also wrote hard-headed dissections of the inefficiency and hence irrationality of housework and childcare being undertaken in isolation; these tasks could be performed more cost-effectively and less wastefully collectively, especially in an age of technological innovation. This argument anticipated Oakley's account of the long hours spent on housework and her assessment of the domestic ideal built around women's confinement to the home. Oakley treated Gilman's literary diatribes against the calamities of military conflict (written during the First World War) and against expensive but unfunctional female fashion garments as perfectly compatible with her sober economic case for a reorganisation of work (including housework) along more co-operative lines. Redirection of military funding could make schemes to improve everyday welfare affordable, for example. The fact that Gilman's best-selling *Women and Economics* was written even more speedily than Oakley's *Sex, Gender and Society* and remained in print decades after its initial publication is another interesting commonality. Gilman was inspired to write this book by visits to the Hull-House Settlement that Jane Addams and Ellen Starr set up in a poor neighbourhood of Chicago to bring practical improvements to the lives of ordinary people and to learn the sociological lessons of those experimental interventions so that they might be adopted elsewhere. Gilman and Addams were exact contemporaries, part of a remarkable generation of pioneering female sociologists who were more predisposed to undertake experimentation in pursuit of what Oakley would later call evidence-based policymaking than were their male counterparts who tended to give abstract theorisation greater priority. Oakley treated settlement sociology with its combination of research and activism as a distinctive type of social science in many ways superior to the traditions that eclipsed it, even if (or perhaps because) what Gilman called the man-made world was not yet ready for it.

The scale of research and practical experimentation into everyday economic and social life described in *Women, Peace and Welfare* forces reconsideration of how the welfare states of the 20th century were created. Oakley noted that many of their best features had their roots in the work of women trailblazers whose piecemeal steps towards addressing the needs of modern industrial societies tend to be overshadowed by the moments of political drama when national schemes were unveiled, even though such schemes would have been inconceivable without their earlier efforts. Oakley's account of these women's endeavours highlights their concern with practicality, seeking to make a difference to the lives of the people whose circumstances many of them found shocking. This shock was especially great for those who came from privileged backgrounds, for whom the squalor and degradation of the poorer neighbourhoods of rapidly expanding cities such as London and Chicago were unlike anything that they had known, but Oakley looked beyond the celebrated philanthropy of the daughters of wealthy families to include the promotion of welfare that women from disadvantaged social situations made. Such women's roots in working-class and minority ethnic backgrounds worked against their appreciation by posterity, notwithstanding the personal insights into women's liberation that they brought, literally so in the case of Ida B Wells who, Oakley noted, had been born into slavery. Oakley argued that Wells should be remembered (amongst many other things) for challenging racially segregated transport seven decades before Rosa Parkes in the 1950s, providing just one example of forgotten precedents for things typically associated with later figures. Thus, Oakley sought to give Katharine Bement Davis due credit for anticipating the approach to studying migration adopted a decade later by W I Thomas in *The Polish Peasant in Europe and America* and Alfred Kinsey's investigation of sexual behaviour a quarter of a century on, while Nellie Bly's covert ethnography of people's treatment in an asylum preceded David Rosenhan's 'On being sane in insane places' by more than eight decades. Even dissemination of findings via prestigious publications such as

the *American Journal of Sociology* did not save these pioneering women from becoming lost to view and with them
their attempts to include topics like sanitation on the social
scientific research agenda.

Many individuals discussed in *Women, Peace and Welfare*
undoubtedly qualified as difficult women, just as Wootton and
the LSE social workers had, but Oakley's use of the adjective
dangerous to describe them conveys the sense of threat that
they were perceived to pose by apologists for the status quo.
This was particularly acute at times of war. During the
Anglo-Boer war, Emily Hobhouse's exposure of the barbarity
of the concentration camps (in which more children died than
fighting men on either side in the conflict) ran counter to the
jingoistic coverage in the British press. She made herself a
nuisance to the authorities with her peace campaigning again
in the First World War. So did many others whose valiant
efforts to end the carnage Oakley's book chronicles. These
women were undeterred by being called traitorous alongside
the insults of hysteria and of being silly, naïve and misguided
to which they were accustomed as familiar responses to efforts
to challenge men's monopoly over public policymaking. They
saw themselves as citizens of the world, opposed to militaristic
nationalism. Nor was these women's perceived dangerousness
restricted to pacifism. Their visions of a good society anticipated a world without the want, disease, squalor, ignorance
and idleness identified later by William Beveridge as the five
giant evils to be tackled by the welfare state. They also looked
beyond these policy agendas by highlighting opportunities
that existed to address women's inferior status and subordination to men in both public and private life. Campaigning for
women's suffrage promised a means of tackling the former
problem more directly than it did the latter, although investigation of how domestic servitude might be escaped through
alternatives   to   conventional   families   had   potential

implications that were similarly subversive. The term 'never married' had been used as an oblique reference to living with another woman in relation to several of Titmuss's social worker colleagues, but this earlier generation included people who were more open about such domestic arrangements. Addams and Mary Rozet Smith, companions of more than 40 years, considered themselves married, for example, while in New York, Lillian Wald, another settlement pioneer, was open about her numerous intimate relationships with women.

Oakley's biography of Wootton did not pursue her subject's sexual orientation, concluding that this is what her subject would have wanted. Wootton's life had involved two heterosexual marriages but also two periods of co-residence with women, Leonora Simeon and Barbara Kyle, involving relationships which she took care to keep private. By contrast, the first wave feminists whose lives Oakley recounts in *Women, Peace and Welfare* included women such as Gilman whose unhappy experience of marriage and motherhood led them not only to chronicle problems associated with the patriarchal family (such as domestic violence) but also to explore and promote alternatives to it. Some did so in both their writings and their personal relationships in which they defied the gender conventions of the day, for example by adopting children as a same-sex couple, by cross-dressing and going by androgynous names. Of the more conventional women who married and stayed with husbands, Oakley was struck by how many had no children, although this did not necessarily free them from expectations that they would be helpmate wives, supporting and putting their husbands' interests first. Marianne Weber (wife of Max) was not restricted to this role and spent more time at the Hull-House Settlement than her husband when they visited Chicago, reflecting her greater interest in the position of women. Yet her own writings are little-known (to monolingual English-speaking researchers, at least) because only her biography of her husband has been translated from the German. Such cases are revealing about how early female social scientists came to be lost from view to subsequent generations. Max Weber's observation about it being the fate of researchers to fade from the consciousness of later scholars has not applied in his case, in part because of the active promotion of his work and memory by the likes of Talcott Parsons (an early translator of Weber's writings). Pioneering female social scientists were rarely championed by established academics, partly because it was harder for these women to hold established academic posts than it was for men (as Wootton had also found). In addition, their research was often actively denigrated by powerful figures as unscientific; such name-calling, however unwarranted, can be very damaging to people's reputations and thereby to their prospects.

Oakley was left reflecting on what might have unfolded had first-wave feminists achieved more recognition and influence through fuller development and application of their ideas during their lifetimes. One important conclusion was that although ideas and practices may be ignored, marginalised, patronised, denigrated or subjected to active efforts to bury them by people who find them threatening, they do not simply disappear. In some cases, they prove resistant to suppression, in others they reappear through rediscovery after a period of having been forgotten, including through the sort of archival work which Oakley had undertaken. Oakley was also led to reflect on how an idea may occur to more than person, either simultaneously or at different moments. She was not the only second wave feminist to discover arguments that she had imagined to be original had already been made by an earlier generation. In methodology, for example, research participants' greater candour when completing questionnaires on their own compared to the answers that they gave in face-to-face interviews was, she realised, well-known to Davis through her study of sexual behaviour; this had been more than six decades before Oakley and her colleagues in the social support and motherhood and young people and family life studies wrote about this issue. It follows that if there are several ways in which ideas and practices come to be forgotten, there will also be various means of setting the historical record straight. In *Social Support and Motherhood*, Oakley had charged Britain's early 20th-century male sociological establishment of appropriating many women's ideas through a process of masculine intellectual colonialism which necessarily involved reworking them so that they fitted into pre-existing sets of assumptions about gendered rationality. Oakley's research for *Women, Peace and Welfare* confirmed the need to expose such misappropriation by revealing original authorship, but it also uncovered the more destructive side of academic engagement whereby the objective is not to lay claim to ideas but to undermine their credibility by maligning, denigrating and ridiculing them. Oakley's analysis implies that had a better reception been given to the early efforts to practise methodological pluralism and innovation, for example, some of the worst excesses of the paradigm wars could conceivably have been avoided.

Speculation about alternative scenarios ran through Oakley's next book, *Forgotten Wives*. This told the stories of how four women's fortunes were shaped by marriage to famous men and reflected on what might have been without their husbands' overshadowing presence in their lives. Oakley pondered whether Charlotte Frances Payne-Townshend would be remembered more favourably had she not married George Bernard Shaw and become 'Mrs G.B.S.'. She was thus conducting a thought experiment about the effect of marriage on women's lives, exploring whether it stops them being seen as people in their own right. While *Women, Peace and Welfare* used archived material to highlight the forces operating in the public and private spheres that led to the history of a

remarkable generation of women's achievements being sup-
pressed, *Forgotten Wives* concentrated on those elements
closest to home in the lives of Payne-Townshend and three
others, Mary Catherine Macaulay (who married Charles
Booth), Jeanette Beveridge (who married Richard Henry
Tawney) and Jessy Thomson Philip (who married William
Beveridge, having previously been married to David Beveridge
Mair, William's cousin). These four individuals were all alive
during the period of 1880–1920 on which *Women, Peace and
Welfare* had focused. Only the oldest of them, Mary Booth,
featured among the women discussed in that book, but by the
end of their lives, they could all point to similarly distinctive
achievements deserving remembrance. Their obscurity to later
generations could not be attributable to limited accomplishments. Nor was it due to an absence of archived material;
Oakley found plenty of evidence of success contained in their
letters, diaries and other papers that was waiting to be dug out
(a term she preferred to plundered) by a dedicated researcher.
And neither could the explanation for their being lost to view
be explained by deficient connectedness, since they did not
lack connections with key figures like Beatrice and Sidney
Webb nor with institutions such as the LSE through which
powerful currents in support of social reform flowed. The
problem lies, rather, in how they came to be seen, first by
many of their contemporaries (both female and male) and
then by historians (again, both female and male) as less
important than their husbands and less deserving of attention.

While researching *Forgotten Wives*, Oakley was reminded of
the question posed sharply by campaigners for women's liberation in 1975, 'Why be a wife?' The question was not a new one,
but some of the objections to marriage made in previous centuries (such as women losing the right to be independent prop-
erty owners when they married) had been addressed by changes
to the law. Others (such as the prevailing assumption that

women were naturally suited to domesticity) had proved more enduring. This was despite the subjects of *Forgotten Wives* and countless other like-minded women demonstrating that marriage did not require them to renounce all claims to distinct personhood. *Forgotten Wives* recounted their numerous independent accomplishments in public life, but it also revealed the pitfalls of being married, of which two stand out. One was that wives can all too easily find their achievements attributed not to them but to their husbands, as was illustrated by Mary Booth's indispensable contributions to the 17-volume *Life and Labour of the People of London* being credited to Charles. The second pitfall was that being married does not remove women's vulnerability to double-bind situations in which they find themselves subject to mutually incompatible pressures; indeed, it may even exacerbate this problem. Noting that Mary Booth and Charlotte Shaw were criticised for their overly modest behaviour while Janet Beveridge and Jeanette Tawney were condemned for expressing themselves too freely, Oakley concluded that wives had an impossibly difficult balance to strike. Thus were these four wives, and innumerable others before and since, led to ponder whether the rationale for their upbringing and education was to be independent or dependent, active or passive, equal or unequal, to speak or be spoken for, to be engaged primarily in the public or private sphere. This multifaceted issue was crystallised in the questions with which Oakley herself had grappled early on in her own marriage and career: why shouldn't married women work, and what counts as 'work' anyway? The fact that three of the forgotten wives (Booth, Beveridge and Tawney) failed to publish the novels that they had written gave them something else in common with the young Oakley and provided one more reason to reflect on what might have been.

7

AUTOBIOGRAPHY, INTERVIEWS, NOVELS, POETRY AND ESSAYS

Ann Oakley's writing encompasses styles ranging from academic monographs and articles to novels, biography and intellectual history to poetry, policy-relevant reports to reflective essays and popular journalism to autobiographical ruminations. The challenge of classifying her work is further complicated when different styles are combined within a single publication. Autobiographical details appear regularly (recalling her teenage encounters with Barbara Wootton, for example), while her biographical works feature policy discussions (such as when various women featuring in *Father and Daughter*, *Women, Peace and Welfare*, *Forgotten Wives* and *The Science of Housework* considered housing problems and solutions). Similarly, sociologists (both real and fictitious) feature frequently in her novels, as do sociological observations and pronouncements, such as those on reproduction in *Matilda's Mistake*. Her 2007 book *Fracture* blurs the boundaries of literary genres by combining the story of her recovery from personal injury with an analysis of the literature on the sociology of the body and a meditation on ageing and loss, all presented accessibly and sprinkled with humour while academic referencing is kept from dominating the text. The book mentions Carolyn Heilbrun, a Professor of English Literature, deciding to write detective fiction under a pseudonym to save her from the judgemental attitudes of purist academic colleagues. Oakley's second published novel, *Only Angels Forget*, was brought out under the pseudonym Rosamund Clay. This followed her first, *The Men's Room*, which was published under her own name and turned into a television series that she said horrified her. For her later novels, she dropped her pseudonym. The most recent, *The strange lockdown life of Alice Henry*, saw her follow both Heilbrun and Jane Rivers (a character in *Scenes Originating in the Garden of Eden*) into detective fiction. Blurring of literary boundaries did not, however, lead Oakley to regard social science and fiction as indistinguishable. She argued instead that social science has the capacity to move beyond novelists' portrayal of individual perceptions of the world by detecting enduring patterns, for example, the deep-seated discrimination that occurs on a society-wide scale and which needs rigorous research methods to investigate and expose it. That said, unless social science embraces the imagination associated with creative writing, it will be unadventurous in the questions that these research methods are deployed to answer and fall short of what Charles Wright Mills called sociological poetry.

Chelly Halsey's autobiography *No Discouragement* noted that his career's focus reflected his own story: his research on social mobility facilitated by education matched his rise from humble beginnings to being an Oxford don who delivered the BBC's 1978 Reith lectures. Halsey's account of his upward mobility from a working-class background resonated with those of his generation whose careers flourished in the decades following the Second World War. Oakley's autobiographical writings had similar resonance with women readers whose trajectories required navigation of new social and economic parameters, in their case those that emerged during the turbulent 1960s. This is not the claim to typicality of women of her generation that the heroine of her first (unpublished) novel wished to make. Oakley's sociological research soon impressed upon her the impossibility of realising such an ambition in a society marked by profound divisions of social class, ethnicity and other glaring inequalities. Even so, many women recognised her descriptions of housework, motherhood, gender and sexism as akin to their own experiences, and some of them contacted her to express gratitude for recasting what they had believed to be uniquely personal troubles as public issues that merited wider attention. Oakley could thus counter the critique of autobiographical writing as egocentric and self-indulgent by arguing that autobiography provides a route to biographical understanding not only for authors but also for their readers; told well, the story of a life can capture the spirit of the age in which that life has been lived. Second wave feminists treated discussion of personal troubles as potentially liberating; this could reveal the extent of shared struggles against adversity, showing that these did not have to be faced alone. Oakley's discussion of postnatal depression was one application of this principle to a taboo subject, her co-written analysis of miscarriage another. Autobiographical writing nevertheless involves difficult decisions about what details of a life to reveal. Oakley's openness about personal matters in *Taking it like a Woman* was a source of discomfort for some readers, as were the book's poignant fictional narratives of episodes in a tangled love affair, the inclusion of which made the book only semi-autobiographical.

Norbert Elias's idea that sociologists confront and even destroy myths implies that their discipline is inevitably unsettling. Subjecting deeply held beliefs to scrutiny makes for uncomfortable reading, such as when family relationships are investigated. From the outset, Oakley's career had involved debunking myths about family life through publications on the myth of motherhood and on women's nature and women's place, but the frank accounts in *Taking it like a Woman* of how she experienced being a daughter, wife and mother endowed the writing with a more immediate quality. It was one thing to draw on interview material to describe how 40 housewives felt about housework or 55 mothers felt about motherhood but quite another to recount vivid first-hand experiences of these things, notwithstanding the two types of accounts containing similar themes of tensions between love and alienation and fortitude and disappointment relative to romanticised expectations of happy families. Oakley revealed that as a child, she was bemused by cultural norms of family life because of the discrepancies between these and her observations of her relatives' behaviour, including that of her parents. Her father's gentleness and her mother's greater readiness to express anger went against the norms of masculine and feminine behaviour, and it was her father to whom she gravitated, describing her relationship with him as the most powerful influence on her life. Indeed, she would later revisit its enduring significance in *Father and Daughter*, having had further time for reflection as well as being able to draw insights from working as his literary executor and from the contents of the suitcase of letters and other material her mother bequeathed to her. The autobiographical reflections contained in *Taking it like a Woman* related to her first four decades. Her decision to write the book was prompted partly by awareness of her own mortality that had arisen through her experience of life-threatening miscarriage and of treatment for cancer, the illness that had caused her father's death. Her mother was still alive when the book was published, and although Oakley expressed hope that its revelations would not be unduly hurtful, she knew that telling the truth comes with such risks.

Taking it like a Woman highlighted the contradictions that pull family members in different directions, making them feel torn and inadequate, at least relative to the unattainable standards that define dutiful daughters, perfect mothers and other idealised fictions. As a daughter, Oakley knew that she was loved and cared about as well as cared for but nevertheless sensed her parents' disappointment in her, feeling herself an awkward intruder in their world. In addition, they gave mixed messages about what ambitions she might pursue in adulthood, particularly about whether marriage and motherhood might be combined with a career commensurate with a university education. Neither parent provided a role model for such a future, except in the negative sense of confirming the unattractiveness of her mother's decision to become a dependent housewife defined by a husband's achievements. Through her parents' marriage and then her own, she came to appreciate that the contradictory relations between a wife and husband bear the imprint not only of their individual personalities but also of gender ideology steering women towards feminine ideals and men masculine ones. Oakley's encounter with feminists during her PhD confirmed that other women also experienced full-time motherhood as a form of imprisonment or enslavement. Moreover, the structures and processes that created women's unhappy dependence had a name: patriarchy. Oakley's account of everyday life with Robin revealed much about them as individuals, including their individual quirks (both endearing and annoying), but it also conveyed how the forces operating on married couples are not fully within their control. Marriage changes people in numerous ways (perceptible and imperceptible) whether they like it or not. The same holds for parenthood, although differently for mothers and fathers. Oakley's autobiographical reflections matched her sociological observations, made in *Subject Women*, that women are defined by their relationships to others (for example, as daughters, wives and mothers) far more extensively than men are. Consequently, women have fewer opportunities to emulate the figure of rational economic man introduced to the undergraduate Oakley but treated with suspicion by her and fellow sociologists as unsustainably individualistic and trans-actional. To use Elias's phraseology he was an implausible 'I' going about his business unencumbered by obligations to and out of balance with the wider group, the 'We'.

Autobiographies are necessarily concerned with identity's individual and collective dimensions. In Oakley's case, she was particularly concerned to understand what makes a woman and what makes a feminist. Simone de Beauvoir's argument that women are not reducible to their biology hel-ped Oakley to formulate her response, although her concern with the issue of womanhood had engaged her long before she absorbed the ideas in *The Second Sex* (which she had been given by a boyfriend on her 16th birthday but read only much later). *Taking it like a Woman* suggested that specifying what makes a woman was at one level quite simple: it could be framed as conformity to the socialising influences of her all-girls school and of her parents regarding expected behav-iour. Diaries and letters from her youth nevertheless reminded her of her predisposition to resist such influences (prompting in the process her appreciation of the value of such documents that would later aid her understanding of her parents, Barbara Wootton and the four protagonists in *Forgotten Wives*). The feminine roles into which girls have traditionally been socialised are essentially passive, but Oakley kicked against efforts to mould her into the sort of person other people wanted her to be, preferring to exercise greater control over her own destiny. It would not be until her later twenties (by which time she was a married mother researching housework) that she considered herself a feminist, although the factors that she identified as leading to this were not only her immediate domestic and career circumstances and the women's liberation group she joined. She also attached importance to the capacity to recognise and contest oppressive social and economic arrangements that her parents as socialists had imbued in her, notwithstanding their greater ambivalence about feminism. The mid-1980s (when *Taking it like a Woman* came out) also saw Oakley continuing to reflect in *What is Feminism?* and in *Telling the Truth about Jerusalem* on what forces shape feminists and whether feminism's goals might be achieved by other means than the revolutionary ones she had espoused a decade earlier in the conclusion to *Housewife*.

Oakley differed from at least some of her contemporaries by seeing no contradiction between the two elements of her self-description as a feminist sociologist. To those who regarded sociology as irredeemably mired in the sexist formulations of its founding fathers and locked into using the tools of the master's house (to use Audre Lorde's phrase), she made the counterclaim that the discipline's fundamental concern with relations between people makes its perspective inherently feminist. She later reinforced this argument by celebrating those women who can justifiably be numbered among the founding figures of sociology alongside the canonical men whose hagiographic treatment she had decried in *The Sociology of Housework*. In addition, she applauded the female sociologists who were developing fields like the sociology of emotions that malestream sociology had previously neglected. And to critics who opined that sociological formulations concerning women's disadvantage and oppression blunted feminism's political edge and its capacity to bring about practical change, Oakley expressed optimism that sociologists could improve women's situation, especially if they were prepared to be innovative, for example, by grounding their analyses more firmly in women's everyday experiences. *Taking it like a Woman* concluded that there was still much to be done to achieve a satisfactory understanding of everyday relationships, in particular women's apparent predisposition to put the needs and interests of others ahead of their own. The transactional view epitomised by rational economic man leaves economists struggling to explain the behaviour of individuals who unselfishly give more than they receive. Oakley's alternative sociological framing of such behaviour in terms of gift-giving, using the concepts of altruism and the collective good, identified an enduring theme in her work. The idea of the gift was discussed, for example, in a 2016 article that reconsidered what passes between interviewees and interviewers, about which she was led to reflect by revisiting her becoming a mother study. Elsewhere the topic of altruism figured in Oakley's account of people's preparedness to take part in medical research, in her analysis of people's (predominantly women's) readiness to undertake poorly paid or unpaid caring work. It also featured in her discussion of what is given in assisted pregnancies and in the global trade in body parts, and in her commentary on altruism as a touchstone in Richard Titmuss's research long before blood donation was used in *The Gift Relationship* to exemplify non-economic giving.

In *Taking it like a Woman*, Oakley reported feeling that she did not properly understand her father, and that consequently her portrayal of him was idealised. A better appreciation of her father's character would give her a clearer sense how she had become the person she was. She went on to explore Titmuss's life before he became a professor in *Man and Wife* and in specialised articles about his involvement in the Eugenics Society and his research work with Marie Meinhardt, the economist refugee from Nazi Germany with whom he and Jerry Morris collaborated (and who in addition provided another example of female academics quickly becoming

forgotten). Bringing out new editions of Titmuss's work provided Oakley with further insights into his career, but it was
not until her mid-sixties (the age at which her father had died)
that work began on *Father and Daughter*. She was by then in a
stronger position to examine their trajectories and profiles for
commonalities and differences. Her experience from 1990 to
2005 of managing the Social Science Research Unit (SSRU)
bore comparison with Titmuss's headship of his London
School of Economics department, for example. Oakley
revealed in an interview how she sought to cultivate in the
SSRU an alternative to the hierarchical academic culture which
to her embodied masculine norms of command and combat,
only to find her efforts misinterpreted as a type of mothering
which she viewed as no more satisfactory than the established
university practices she sought to supersede. This experience
allowed her to re-evaluate her father's dealings with his female
social work colleagues that had proved so trying to both
parties. She reflected more generally on how social scientists
operate within gendered frameworks that are hard to dislodge.
Father and Daughter brought home just how much of her
father's intellectual perspective Oakley had taken on, including
his scepticism regarding medical ideology, his preparedness to
write about his personal experience of medical encounters, his
awareness of the negative consequences of social class
inequalities, his aversion to pretentious theoretical writing and
his capacity to think beyond disciplinary boundaries. Writing
the book also made her aware of how not all of her father's
ways of looking at the world were shared; her greater interest
in and radically different views on sex and gender provided the
most obvious area of generational discontinuity.

Oakley's understanding of relations between members of
succeeding generations was shaped by Mills's encouragement
to sociologists to bring together biography, history and social
structure and by her further interests in people's disposition

and temperament. The social structures in which she and her father had grown up were markedly different, notably because in the interim the Beveridge Report had been published; its implementation during Oakley's childhood created a comprehensive welfare state about which the young Richard could only have dreamt. Oakley's education extended until she left university with a degree aged 21; by contrast, her father left school at 14 with no qualifications, being required by his family to bring in an income. In addition, the social conservatism of the interwar years in which he became an adult contrasted with the progressive 1960s when she came of age. That decade challenged many of the certainties of her father's generation, not least the assumptions made about relations between women and men. Her father's principal focus on social class inequalities and relatively limited interest in women's disadvantaged position reflected his generation, but it was also the product of his core academic social network being predominantly male-oriented. His links to Baroness Wootton and to his LSE department's social workers notwithstanding, Titmuss was more engaged by and worked most closely with the men whom he appointed, notably Brian Abel-Smith, Peter Townsend and David Donnison. This group of social policy experts which Titmuss assembled was described by Oakley as a boys' network in a conscious echo of the so-called girls' network of social workers with whom Titmuss clashed. This does not, however, convey the complexity of the group's dynamics because the younger men's attraction to Titmuss was not only as an intellectual father figure but also contained an unspoken erotic element. Oakley's recall of her mother's agonised disclosure of her father cross-dressing and her own discovery through archival material of his unresolved sense of betrayal by Townsend's departure from LSE to lead the University of Essex's new Department of Sociology revealed further sides to the man at odds with his public image, in the process highlighting the complexity of memory and the unstable character of social networks.

Oakley's networks have never resembled those associated with the Eugenics Society and the LSE that were pivotal for Titmuss's career progress. Individuals who have had an enduring influence on her (such as her father) can be identified, but they do not share sufficiently strong mutual connections to form an integrated network; although her social connectedness is extensive, it is by comparison much more compartmentalised. *Father and Daughter* described Oakley's acquaintance with her father's colleagues, but she remained outside their academic collaborations, and their influence on her was latent, for example, through their discussions of the relative merits of quantitative and qualitative methods. It was, likewise, only after Wootton's death that Oakley embarked on her biography. Acknowledgements to Robin Oakley appear in her publications throughout her career, but they were co-authors only once. Iain Chalmers, whom she discovered had been taught by her father's colleague Jerry Morris, has been a powerful influence since their first meeting in 1975. Chalmers's effect on her thinking about experimental methods endured long after her move a decade later to the Thomas Coram Research Unit coincided with the end of her formal association with his National Perinatal Epidemiological Unit. The Cochrane Collaboration that Chalmers set up in 1993 was enormously influential for the work on systematic reviewing undertaken by the EPPI Centre during Oakley's time as Director of the SSRU (within which it was located), but their last joint publication predated that. Overall, Oakley has nearly as many joint publications as she does single-authored ones, but rather than overlapping her co-authors fall into discrete groups. Things co-written with Sandy Oliver, David Gough, Angela Harden, James Thomas and many other EPPI Centre colleagues constitute a substantial body of work, but they are concentrated in the EPPI Centre's first decade and relate primarily to Oakley's interest in evaluation. Her collaborative edited collections with Juliet Mitchell concerning developments in feminism spanned three decades, as did her projects with Helen Roberts. Both collaborations show that working together does not require a shared institutional base or a fixed one (given that Oakley's earlier career involved frequent relocation). Oakley has, however, consistently lamented the demerits of short-term contracts with which researchers must contend; crucial among these drawbacks are the obstacles to career building, including the unevenness of access to networks that lies at the root of that process being gendered.

Father and Daughter brought greater clarity than Oakley had possessed 30 years earlier when many questions about who she was and what she might become remained unresolved. Writing the book was especially enlightening about how she was her father's daughter in some ways by choice (for example, pursuing a career in academia), while in others, her inheritance was involuntary (such as her physical resemblance to him); furthermore, some similarities were accompanied by differences (such as her rejection of her father's medicalised solution to the insomnia from which they both suffered). The book also facilitated observations about the challenges of biographical and autobiographical writing, notably the unreliability and incompleteness of memory. Her discussion cast doubt on nostalgic recollections and raised the possibility of memories being fictional or suppressed. Her childhood polio was long forgotten until an unrelated medical examination more than 60 years later prompted the memory to resurface. Related reflections on memory featured in *Fracture*, where the vagaries of medical record keeping were explored. The operation to repair her arm was followed by extensive medical consultations, accounts of which erroneously recorded which arm had suffered the fracture and mis-typed her weight as 233 pounds (which placed her in the morbidly obese category), not the 133 it should have been. Less easily rectifiable was the focus in the doctors' notes on measurable physiological function and the corresponding neglect of the sensations of pain and numbness that she experienced that were harder to demonstrate. This experience aligned with what interviewees reported in Oakley's becoming a mother study, that doctors do not always engage with what their patients tell them. A further echo of that study lay in the idea of major bodily changes (such as those associated with pregnancy and childbirth) being associated with biographical disruption. Oakley's expertise in medical sociology had acquainted her with the idea that the stories people tell about their lives include episodes of changed direction in which adjustments to their sense of self must be made because previous understandings prove unsustainable. The awareness that Oakley's injury prompted of bodily capacities being lost (and of ageing more generally) constituted one such episode.

Alongside the theme of loss in *Fracture* is the contrasting narrative of liberation from the myth of the perfect body. Pressure to pursue impossibly high standards of bodily perfection for young people and resignation to the prospect of inevitable deterioration associated with ageing were equally objectionable. She cited findings that one in five girls worry about their weight by the age of five, and that two in five are dieting by the age of nine, while also arguing that postmenopausal women are subject to pressures to retire their bodies from public view once they no longer have a reproductive function and develop flaws. According to medical definitions, it is unusual for postmenopausal women to have normal bone density, but Oakley endeavoured to reduce her risk of fractures not through widely promoted medication but by keeping fit, treating exercise (including taking up ballet and making cycling her preferred mode of transport) as a better way of avoiding deteriorating skeletal health. Oakley had long been sceptical of the medicalisation of the menopause, notably the idea that women's bodies need medical science's help to adjust to a natural process. In *Experiments in Knowing*, she expressed doubts about the extensive range of allegedly menopausal symptoms; it smacked of pharmaceutical salespeople touting hormone replacement therapy as a solution for middle-aged women experiencing tiredness, insomnia, weight gain, irritability, headaches, depression and numerous other familiar conditions that quite possibly had other causes. Attributing these symptoms to oestrogen deficiency would be more convincing, Oakley argued, if they were not also commonly reported by men of a similar age. Moreover, in some cultures women aged over 50 are regarded positively. The wise women forerunners of professional midwives and other female lay healers about whom Oakley wrote in her becoming a mother study and in her book with Suzanne Houd *Helpers in Childbirth* were often older community members valued for their expertise. And in contrast to the negative stereotype of old age found in supposedly more advanced societies, Oakley presented the idea of opportunities associated with accumulated wisdom and the freedom that comes from no longer being beholden to other people's expectations about appearance and behaviour. Alice Henry, the 74-year-old heroine of Oakley's 2022 novel, exemplified this approach to life.

Several of Oakley's books (*Man and Wife, Gender on Planet Earth, Fracture, A Critical Woman, Father and Daughter, Women, Peace and Welfare* and *Forgotten Wives*) discuss Virginia Woolf's use of novels, essays and other literary forms to capture women's inferior place in society. Oakley mentioned Woolf's essay on time when introducing her poems about this in *Telling the Truth about Jerusalem*. Later in that book, Woolf's theme of women's outsider status in a man's world is echoed in Oakley's poem General Smuts Pub. This conveyed her experience of being surrounded by policemen and football fans on a match night in west London, revealing how patriarchal arrangements are simply taken for granted by men, leaving her feeling like she belonged to another planet. Conversely, women who have self-confidence are all too aware of how patriarchy revolves around processions of men from which they and other females are excluded, thereby having their imagination fired to consider how the social world might be reordered so that women are not located as outsiders. Episodes of gender crossing provide one means of prompting such considerations in Woolf's *Orlando* and in Oakley's *The strange lockdown life of Alice Henry*. Oakley was less persuaded by the dim view Woolf took of methodically collected evidence as inferior to fiction but was impressed by her preparedness to experiment with new forms of writing such as *Three Guineas*, her angry polemic against war and patriarchy, even though something more akin to her previous work would have been better received by critics. Woolf's arguments in *Three Guineas* about people's common interests were the starting point of *Gender on Planet Earth*. Oakley also concurred with Woolf's suggestion that women's socialisation into subordinate roles engenders in them powers of observation that facilitate novel writing based on personal experience, although the manifestation of this subordination in the altruistic self-sacrifice idealised by the Victorians would need to be overcome if the time to write such novels were ever to materialise. This theme of Woolf's in *A Room of One's Own* was echoed in Oakley's various references to the rural retreat where much of her writing since the late 1980s (including various novels) has been done.

Oakley's observation that Woolf and other novelists drew on personal experience also applied to herself. The setting of *Scenes*

Originating in the Garden of Eden resembles the location of her rural retreat, just as there are parallels to her own life in the adjustments to living away from the city made in adulthood by Flora Penfold (its main protagonist). The novel's storyline drew additionally on familiar ideas. At the beginning of the novel, Flora's predicament as a woman sensing that her current life was unfulfilling and lacking meaning updated to the 1990s the question that Betty Friedan's archetypal American housewife of the 1960s had lain awake pondering, 'Is that all there is?' The country characters include a village doctor who was knowledgeable about randomised controlled trials and other villagers who could have stepped out of the pages of the community studies that Oakley encountered earlier in her career (when the richness of the fieldwork on which they reported led her to describe them as a veritable fishpond). There is relatively little about housework in the novel, but issues of reproduction (seduction, copulation, pregnancy, miscarriage, abortion, infertility and sexually transmitted disease) loom large, informed by her medical sociology expertise. Flora's remark about how fewer than 10% of human conceptions result in a live birth provides an example of a fictional character sharing her academic knowledge. Oakley's research and everyday observations also inform sub-plots dealing with sexual harassment, cross-dressing, music appreciation, psychotherapy and an academic father about whom Flora discovered things that were previously secret through coming into possession of his personal papers after his death. The book was dedicated to Kay and Richard Titmuss, and Flora's reflections on people being denied opportunities resonated with Oakley's mother's frustrated writing ambitions (in contrast to Flora's mother fulfilling hers). It also resonated with Oakley's father having to leave his treasured rural roots, the value of which Oakley appreciated only in adulthood. Flora's realisation that rural life is less than idyllic but still attractive was aided by producing a cartoon series whose central character, Rosey, becomes an alter ego through whom greater self-knowledge can be gleaned, just as novel-writing allowed Oakley to explore ideas from different angles.

Oakley noted in *Women Confined* that it was dangerous to generalise based on individual accounts of difficult experiences but that they nevertheless can generate sociological insights. In her novels, many of the characters face predicaments illustrating Mills's axiom that personal troubles connect to public issues. Like Flora Penfold, the lead protagonists of Oakley's other novels (Charity Walton in *The Men's Room*, Matilda Cressey in *Matilda's Mistake*, Eleanor Jenkinson in *The Secret Lives of Eleanor Jenkinson*, Dodo Delancey in *A Proper Holiday*, Lydia Mallinder in *Overheads*, Alice Henry in *The strange lockdown life of Alice Henry* and Isobel Kargar in the pseudonymously published *Only Angels Forget*) all struggle with relational challenges. Family members and other intimates such as husbands and other partners (and ex-husbands and ex-partners), fathers, mothers, siblings, sons and daughters are prominent among the cast of characters with whom they engage, along with work colleagues, health professionals, neighbours, friends, passing acquaintances and strangers (such as the flasher Flora encountered in *Scenes Originating in the Garden of Eden*). Tensions relating to unreconciled gendered expectations feature in many of these relationships, sometimes those between women characters (as when mothers and daughters disagree about caring responsibilities and other notions of appropriate behaviour that have shifted across generations) but more often between the female lead protagonists and men suffering from self-centredness, excessive ambition, insufficient seriousness, deceitfulness or another unsympathetic characteristic. These failings were sufficiently numerous to prompt a figure in *The Men's Room* to rework Friedan's famous aphorism by entitling her paper 'Men: The Problem With Too Many Names'. In *Scenes Originating in the Garden of Eden*, one of these names is misogyny. Hatred of women is an extreme expression of a more general malaise of masculinity being brought into crisis by social changes that feminism helped to usher in. In the management of personal welfare research programme, Oakley and her colleagues voiced dissatisfaction with the attribution of behaviour around violence, delinquency and the unequal distribution of caring responsibilities to men's biological make-up. Biological difference remained an important reference point for those promulgating the backlash against feminism's challenge, and these debates provided an important backdrop for Oakley's novels' plotlines as women and men sought less conflictual and more sustainable ways of coexisting.

Quotations from de Beauvoir's *The Second Sex* prefaced each chapter of *The Men's Room*, highlighting the difficulties faced by women seeking to be independent, equal and authentic in a masculine universe while at the same time avoiding isolation and the undue costs of altruism. Significantly, the novel's principal character was called Charity. De Beauvoir and Oakley both resisted the self-denial that their mothers expected (not least because they knew that these same mothers had been embittered by the personal sacrifices associated with devotion to their families). They were, nevertheless, mindful that a woman's decision not to organise her life around men might also damage her well-being. De Beauvoir's ideas do not feature in Oakley's earliest works but figure prominently later on. Just as the varied styles of Woolf, Gilman and Wootton provided inspiration, Oakley appreciated the diverse literary forms through which the French thinker and activist analysed women's otherness when men and men's experiences are presumed to be the norm. In *Fracture*, Oakley drew on De Beauvoir's book *Old Age* when disputing that older women were like housework, invisible and not worth studying. The passage in de Beauvoir's autobio-graphical *Memoirs of a Dutiful Daughter* in which she described how she knew her mother too well to regard her as saintly featured in *Subject Women* and was echoed in Oakley's analyses of her relationship with her father. References to *The Second Sex* abound in Oakley's textbook (for example, in discussions of women dressing for show, of the enriching nature of mother-hood and of paid employment offering the best route by which women might escape dependency and parasitism). Oakley's knowledge of the findings of archival research and of de Beau-voir's novel *She Came to Stay* allowed her to question the con-ventional wisdom that emphasised de Beauvoir's intellectual debt to her partner (the existentialist philosopher Jean-Paul Sartre) while downplaying the impact of her ideas on him. And Oakley used de Beauvoir's *Adieux: A Farewell to Sartre* as the starting point of an essay on feminism and knowledge in which the focus on rational man is argued to be deficient because of its exclusion of women's ways of knowing involving affec-tivity, emotions and sensibility to others' needs.

The essay form allows greater freedom of expression than monographs and journal articles that use more formulaic means to report findings of research projects. Many of Oakley's essays in *Telling the Truth about Jerusalem* and *Essays on Women, Medicine and Health* rework conference presentations, giving them a freer, more discursive quality that feeds readers' imagi-nation. This was true, for example, of the essay in the latter collection that began with Sartre's ruminations about planetary satellites that placed him at the centre of things and concluded with a limerick about a housewife defying the gravitational pull of the dull routines of her life with her husband. The chapters of *Gender on Planet Earth* also have an essay-like quality to them, though they constitute an integrated whole through their elab-oration of its core theme of aliens and outsiders (which had been the book's provisional title). Here, Oakley experimented with unusual forms of authorship, including imagining what reviewers might make of her book. (In the prefaces to new editions of her publications, her discussion of previous reviewers' comments revealed a keen interest in how her work was received.) Several chapters revisited familiar themes. One on cycling elaborated on the dangers of being forced to compete for road space with London drivers by recounting in detail a particularly eventful journey. *Man and Wife* had concluded by describing a similar adventure, but this time, she highlighted the gendered nature of the experience about which she knew through reading Wootton's analysis of motoring offences as a predominantly male preserve. This contrasts strikingly with Flora Penfold's car-free rural cycle ride in *Scenes Originating in the Garden of Eden*, but the conclusion drawn by Oakley was not about the evils of urbanism but rather about patriarchal processes. Car culture embodies patriarchal thinking and pushes women and cyclists (and especially women cyclists) to the margins. It is so normalised as to be unremarkable, even though the individual and environmental costs of car dependency cry out for attention. Tellingly, it was a woman who was Britain's first pedestrian killed by a car, but despite the enthusiasm around that time of first-wave feminists for cycling and notwithstanding the subsequent demonstration of cycling's health benefits, bicycles have been thoroughly out-competed by cars.

Another chapter in *Gender on Planet Earth* relates Oakley's encounter with a man who indecently exposed himself and verbally and physically harassed her. This episode came some years after writing about a flasher in *Scenes Originating in the Garden of Eden* and was altogether more threatening. It was further along the continuum of misogynistic behaviour that Oakley treated as starting with jokes and ending with murder, noting in the process the typographical closeness of manslaughter and man's laughter. Like the figures for traffic-related fatalities, those for gender-based murders were shocking: data for England

and Wales revealed a third of female homicide victims were killed by a former or current partner, while in the United States, the commonest cause of death during pregnancy was murder, most usually by the woman's partner. Other US data showed pregnancy to be when women are most at risk of domestic violence, with additional danger to the fetus. The work of her friend Cynthia Cockburn was used by Oakley to support the proposition that women typically prefer words to weapons as means of resolving conflicts, thereby raising concerns about the problematic consequences of masculinity and its violent expression in various situations (including warfare) from which both men and women end up suffering. Masculinity's negative effects for people of both genders also emerged from the chapter devoted to family life, aspects of which men as well as women can find alienating. The fact that significantly more petitions for divorce are filed by wives may reflect their experience of femininity as an obstacle to achieving active selfhood, but Oakley argued that ideals of masculinity as power and dominance also constitute obstacles to fulfilling relationships. For different reasons, everybody loses until such time as new, more emotionally intelligent ways of managing relationships within families emerge. Oakley's reflections on her relationships with her grandchildren (the first of whom was born in the late 1990s) being infinitely more rewarding than the distant ones she had with her grandparents or that her parents had with her children offer some encouragement regarding the possibilities of reaching such a future relatively quickly, albeit that grandfathers typically have further to travel.

In an interview, Oakley expressed disappointment at the relatively muted reception of *Gender on Planet Earth*. Her bold ambition had been to highlight interconnections between the multiplicity of crises unfolding on a global scale (including environmental, health and economic ones) and gender inequality. Her preceding essay in *Who's Afraid of Feminism?* provided the foundation for this analysis by offering a history of gender in the quarter century since she and others began using the term with the aim of properly understanding phenomena wrongly attributed to supposedly natural sex differences. The ensuing debates between competing strands of feminist thinking frequently returned to the issue of how culture related to nature and biology which had prompted her to write *Sex, Gender and Society*. She defended the continued use of the concept of gender against criticisms from different angles, not only those of biological determinists looking to attribute inequalities to people's nature but also those of feminists who were disappointed that the concept had delivered little to counter men's power and women's oppression. In addition to offering theoretical critiques of these various positions, a key element in Oakley's response related to their questionable relationship to evidence. The exhaustive research material adduced meant that this shortcoming could not be associated with *Gender on Planet Earth*. The book's reflections on the prospects for a world without gender were reinforced by relaying what could be learned from studies of animal rearing practices, vegetarianism, cigarette smoking, sport, female genital mutilation, men's liberation, militarism, bonfire night rituals, gossip, science fiction, the biosphere, genetic engineering, racism, individualism, capitalism, shopping and numerous other topics. Oakley's analysis led once again to the need to challenge myths, a task that she considered may be easier for women and other minority groups at the margins of a male-dominated society. There were, however, exceptions to the contention that men are less curious about their position than women are theirs, two such being Jeff Hearn, who worked with her to analyse men's problematic presence in welfare policies, and Martin Holbeach, a character in the novel *A Proper Holiday* who was sufficiently conversant with the debate about sex and gender to expound on Oakley's pioneering ideas.

8

ANN OAKLEY'S LEGACY

The story of Oakley's career is revealing about how her thinking evolved. In addition to providing a compelling narrative of sustained personal accomplishment, it also illustrates how public and private influences shape a lifetime's work and how an individual scholar's contribution to a discipline can endure. Sociology has changed enormously since Oakley, the prospective research student, struggled to find a supervisor who shared her enthusiasm for investigating housework; the Economic and Social Research Council's (ESRC) inclusion of her PhD among the most significant projects that it has funded, her recognition by the UK Data Service and the British Library as a pioneering social researcher and her receipt of the British Sociological Association (BSA) lifetime achievement award all attest that her doggedness paid off both to her benefit and social science's. The ubiquity of the concept of gender in contemporary discourse also indicates how different the world was when Oakley wrote *Sex, Gender and Society*, seeking to untangle the muddled thinking concerning what could be attributed to biological sex differences and what to cultural influences. Few first books have such a dramatic impact; those it quickly surpassed included, coincidentally, that by Bryan

Wilson (the Oxford don who taught her sociological theory) which was entitled, apparently unselfconsciously, *Sects and Society*. Oakley's interests led her to engage with diverse topics, which *The Ann Oakley Reader* grouped under four headings: sex and gender; housework and family life; childbirth, motherhood and medicine; and doing social science. These themes were not studied discretely or consecutively; instead, Oakley's career trajectory saw her engaging with developments in thinking about sex and gender in various publications including the three collections edited with Juliet Mitchell and in *Gender on Planet Earth*. She also returned repeatedly to the study of motherhood and in the process reflected periodically on epistemological disputes about knowledge claims and the nature of science. She has in addition revisited frequently the subject of her starting point, housework; most recently, *The Science of Housework* has much to say about domestic labour and women's preparation for it, just as *Forgotten Wives*, *Women, Peace and Welfare*, *Father and Daughter*, *Gender on Planet Earth*, *Social Support and Motherhood*, *Subject Women* and (in a rather different style) *Taking it like a Woman* had also. Oakley's new introduction to the 2019 edition of *The Sociology of Housework* noted that housework research progressed markedly in the 45 years following its original publication, but she also observed that the finding that housework falls mainly onto women has remained stubbornly enduring.

Oakley has consistently emphasised the importance of the research questions to which answers are sought because so much rests on researchers formulating them well. The types of research questions that Oakley has posed can be treated as rooted in four fundamental challenges to social scientists: first, to explore who we are (an identity issue); secondly, to determine who gets what (a distributional issue that is often associated with matters of conflict); thirdly, to investigate whether people can live together more or less peaceably (an issue of social integration and conflict resolution); and fourthly, to judge the veracity of knowledge claims (a methodological and philosophical issue). In relation to the first issue, much of Oakley's research has explored what it means to be a woman, focusing on the meaning of wifedom (for example, as housewives) and motherhood both now and in the past. The second issue encompasses her work on how women occupy inferior economic, political and social positions relative to men and the role of gender ideologies in reproducing these inequalities and of the feminist movement in challenging them. The third issue relates to what Oakley says about people living together harmoniously or otherwise at the micro level (for example, women and men or parents and children in families) and, at the macro level, about citizens of whole societies being more or less co-operative and helped or hindered in the pursuit of co-operation by public policy and by rituals and myths. The fourth issue arises because of the disputatious nature of social science, which Oakley's early challenge to malestream thinking illustrated, as did the paradigm wars into which she was inevitably drawn by her preference for methodological pluralism over methodolatry. The four broad challenges confirm Oakley's preparedness to cross disciplinary boundaries, taking her beyond sociology to engage, respectively, with psychology, medicine and sociobiology, with economics and social policy analysis, with social anthropology and politics and with philosophy and education. Furthermore, Oakley's engagement with history runs throughout her work, illuminating change and continuity in housework and motherhood and in the ebbs and flows that characterise both methodological debate and feminism's successive waves. An additional interdisciplinary feature of Oakley's work relates to literature and her experimentation with different writing genres while searching for the most appropriate means of engaging diverse audiences with her ideas; among other things, well-crafted research questions will facilitate such experimentation.

Oakley's interest in identity began early as she strove to understand what her parents, her teachers and other people around her wanted her to be and why such expectations were sometimes difficult to meet. The moulding of women's identities through their relationships with others (for example, as dutiful daughters, helpmate wives, caring mothers and supportive sisters, both literal and metaphorical) reflects the constraining presence of patriarchal ideology that was scrutinised in *Subject Women*, her wide-ranging analysis of women's subjection in male-dominated societies. This followed Charles Wright Mills's exhortation of sociologists to ask what kinds of people are present in particular societies. He argued that the types of men and women to be found are not fixed by some immutable human nature but vary according to compelling historical forces and biographical influences. The influence of Simone de Beauvoir's *The Second Sex* (which Mills had reviewed enthusiastically, albeit with some criticisms) can thus be detected in *The Sociological Imagination*'s ambition to help people achieve a better understanding of themselves, even if he did periodically slip into using the words man and men generically to include women. Oakley continued to ponder the forces that had shaped her own identity. In *Father and Daughter*, her self-description mentioned the recognition she received through her work on gender, housework, childbirth, research methodology, biography, autobiography, policy analysis and novel writing, including assessments (such as the critical reception of her championing of experimental social science) that she would rather not have had. She used Peter Marris's likening of identity to a clothes horse on which items are draped to highlight that when individuals present themselves to the world, they are mindful of the expectations of the people and the norms of the institutions around them; estimation and classification by others helps to confirm a person's sense of self or, less happily, undermine it. What a person is taught, encouraged, pressed or cajoled to be may not always feel right, and Oakley's experiences of doing good but feeling bad and her observation of this phenomenon amongst others led her to reflect on the embodied nature of emotions and how this may vary with gender, although not necessarily aligning with stereotypes of how men and women handle emotions. *Subject Women* discussed the differences between the styles of male and female writers of fiction and non-fiction including their recourse to emotional language, noting that research did not confirm stereotypical expectations about male writers being more logical and women writers more verbose.

The usefulness of greater understanding of emotions for the development of women's self-awareness is an important theme in Oakley's novels, being particularly prominent in the internal conversations that the heroines of *Scenes Originating in the Garden of Eden* and *The Secret Lives of Eleanor Jenkinson* have with their alter egos (Rural Rosey and Esther Gray, respectively). Fiction allowed the latter to facilitate Eleanor's expression of what being her felt like, offering a description reminiscent of Betty Friedan's unnamed problem of dissatisfaction with apparently ideal family life. Consideration of emotions in non-fiction also aids understanding the social world because, as Oakley noted in *Experiments in Knowing*, knowledge claims are made by real people complete with emotional resources and baggage, not robotic practitioners of objective science. The preface to *From Here To Maternity* related the mixed emotions (including intense joy but also bewilderment and fear) that she experienced on becoming a mother, while *Taking it like a Woman* referred to feelings of exhaustion and incapability. These observations informed readers about the person who later asked other new mothers about what childbirth had been like for them. This linked to her desire, mentioned in her chapter on interviewing women, to give something back to her interviewees, despite such emotion work going against textbook norms of the time about how researchers should behave. The idea that women benefitted from greater emotional support during pregnancy and early motherhood was investigated in the social support and motherhood research, although the findings of this and other projects were disappointing in that the arrival of children did not alter emotional support in families being treated as women's work. Engagement with emotions of a different sort arose when Oakley wrote her biography of Barbara Wootton, whom she admired but did not like. Oakley traced the roots of the latter sentiment back to her childhood encounters with her father's rather forbidding colleague, and although her research taught her much more about Wootton, she still did not warm to her subject. A similar ambivalence featured in her assessment of Richard Titmuss in *Father and Daughter* where her deep filial love sat uncomfortably alongside her dislike of his argumentativeness, outbursts of temper and emotional inarticulacy in the private realm of the family which ran counter to the man's saintly reputation. The bravery of Oakley's preparedness to share details of the emotional journeys associated with her research projects has contributed to greater openness among social scientists when presenting their findings.

Oakley's principal legacy in relation to the sociological understanding of identity relates to the uncoupling from their biological make-up of who women are as people. Her early exposition in *Sex, Gender and Society* of the distinction between sex as biology and gender as culture was formulated as she developed her critique of the idea that low status activities such as housework were naturally part of women's domain, and the related notion that a woman's place is in the home. Her argument that there is nothing natural about the allocation of domestic tasks to women was compelling and quickly became accepted sociological wisdom. Challenging the idea of women having natural roles was more straightforward when considering housework than it was in relation to Oakley's subsequent research topic, motherhood. By the time Oakley wrote *Subject Women*, she was arguing that it was erroneous for biology be taken as a given because of the various ways in which what is perceived to be nature can be shown to be affected by nurture; in consequence, biology and culture are not always as easily distinguished as her initial formulation had suggested. She later reflected that she and other feminists in the 1970s were focused on using the concept of gender to challenge widespread assumptions about women's positions in society being innate. Oakley's book *Fracture* and the Introduction to the 2015 edition of *Sex, Gender and Society* retained as their key starting point the bold statement that people's (men's as well as women's) selves are not reducible to their bodies. Over time, however, her awareness grew of how bodily and cultural processes are interwoven in the reproduction of women's subordination. The fact that women are twice as likely as men to be pre-scribed mood-altering drugs, the remarkable rise in the use of caesarean sections to the point at which they are in parts of the world becoming the normal mode of childbirth, and the similarly remarkable emergence of hormone replacement therapy as a multi-billion dollar industry aimed at post-menopausal women all offer stark illustrations of how women's bodies are sites of extensive medical interventions. Such interventions complicate the changes to the sense of self associated with becoming a mother or going through the menopause; Oakley also reported experiencing biographical disruption due to the fracture of her right arm that she suffered.

Oakley's remark in *Fracture* that her approach to theoris-ing starts with personal experience is exemplified by the investigations that she undertook into phenomena of which she had first-hand knowledge (such as housework, mother-hood and medical interventions), but she did not restrict herself to writing only about things she had experienced directly. She drew usefully on the academic economist Deirdre McCloskey's perceptive memoir of her gender transition, for example, noting that the experience of gender crossing brings particularly vivid insights into masculine and feminine identity formation. Among other things, such narratives reinforce the point which Oakley made repeatedly, that gender is key to understanding not only women's situation but also men's. McCloskey's account in *Crossing* resonates with Oakley's long-standing theme about the alienating consequences for men of pursuing masculine ideals. Where dedication to rationality hampers engagement with one's emotions and where competitive individualism makes relationships with others transactional, shallow and prone to violence then masculinity's association with powerful positions and material advantages can be judged to come at too high a cost. Oakley's argument that avoiding the traps of conventional expressions of gender is in men's interests as well as women's encouraged male academics to explore the potential of men's studies. Masculinity as a subject of investigation was slower to emerge than women's studies, but pioneers such as David Morgan (who was the sole male contributor to Helen Roberts's edited collection on feminist research to which Oakley had contributed) stimulated and consolidated its momentum. By the time of the 1990s research initiative (with which Oakley had been involved) that had the edited collection *Men, Gender Divisions and Welfare* as one of its principal publications evidence was accumulating that feminists' challenge to men to think through the implications of the concept of gender for their position was bearing fruit. In *Taking It Like A Woman*, Oakley disputed the charge that feminists were necessarily men-haters. *Gender on Planet Earth* developed the theme that men and women share an interest in moving towards social relationships in which gender has decreasing prominence, even if the journey away from gender inequalities was undeniably a long-term project. Taking stock of feminism's achievements, Oakley's conclusion remained that there had been too little change, not (as promulgators of the backlash asserted) too much.

Oakley's interest in gender identity leads on to the question 'who gets what?' Her doctoral study had highlighted not only that housewives were not paid for doing housework but also that it typically took up most of their waking hours (and considerably longer than a standard full-time employment contract). Only a minority of the young mothers who were interviewed for the study undertook paid work, but in *Subject Women*, Oakley reviewed research findings that compared the labour market positions of men and women. These showed that gender mattered to the pay and conditions enjoyed by employees, more or less universally to women's disadvantage. This related, in turn, to the caring responsibilities that fell primarily to women. Oakley's study of becoming a mother highlighted how the arrival of children changed the dynamics in married couples' relationships, and her later investigation with Julia Brannen and colleagues into families with teenage children showed that emotional labour constituted an equally enduring element of women's caring responsibilities alongside practical caring tasks within households, with men as well as children the principal beneficiaries; by contrast, women suffered poorer health as a result. In addition to directing attention to the many forms of unpaid labour as arenas of gender inequality, Oakley also pointed to other fields in which unequal outcomes result from gendered processes. Her own experiences as a daughter and pupil had shown that parents and teachers convey different messages to boys and girls about their prospective futures, for example, with girls having to defy stereotypical expectations of passivity and dependence if they are to realise their full potential. The cultural association of femininity with passive compliance was particularly striking for Oakley in her observations of doctor–patient interactions in the becoming a mother study, and much of her subsequent research highlighted the costs to women's health of what she regarded as their disempowerment or even infantilisation by medical professionals. The overall picture presented by Oakley is of women as a subordinate group in societies that operate according to masculine norms that are so entrenched as to seem unremarkable. In a man's world, women's second-class status is frequently overlooked by people in positions of power, and women's activities are vulnerable to being downgraded, sometimes to the point of invisibility, as Oakley's housework study demonstrated. She showed more generally that such double standards are integral to unequal outcomes along gender lines and to the repro-duction of anti-women societies.

Oakley's message about gender inequality is that it is deep-rooted but nevertheless susceptible to change. Her work featured historical analysis from the outset, emphasising that women's and men's roles are far from fixed; the housewife dependent on the male breadwinner was a relatively recent creation, for example, emerging out of a particular phase of the industrial revolution and subject to all manner of variations in different contexts. Further changes to women's economic dependence unfolded in the second half of the 20th century as wives' employment became increasingly common and welfare state agencies provided levels of support generous by historical standards, although elements of this support were vulnerable to reversal through political shifts, as Oakley's periodic stock-taking exercises revealed. By the end of the century, second-wave feminism had enhanced awareness of opportu-nities to challenge women's disadvantaged situation, given how differently things had stood merely three decades previously when the women's liberation movement began realigning the terms of the conversation about gender inequality. Campaigning for women patients' voices to be taken more seriously by the medical establishment provided a good example of what practical feminism has the potential to achieve but also of the distance still to be travelled. More broadly, Oakley's historical research showed how agendas for change wax and wane. This led to the salutary observation that several ambitions of second-wave feminists contained echoes of things for which their predecessors in the first wave had struggled only for these campaigns to be subsequently lost to view. Indeed, the alternative visions of future social relations that inspired figures in *Women, Peace and Welfare* included projects (such as Charlotte Perkins Gilman's kitchenless home) that were striking in their imaginativeness by the standards of any era. Consciously or otherwise, later generations of women confronted by the conundrum of how to break free from domesticity were revisiting the quest of Gilman and her contemporaries to overcome the barriers that stand in the way of engaging in the public sphere as men's equals. Even if formal obstacles to women's advancement (such as the male monopoly over appointment to the House of Lords) had been removed in Wootton's lifetime, the belittlement of women as less capable than men is a cultural phenomenon which continues to be familiar, as is the potential for public spaces to be intimidating because of threats of objectification, harassment and violence.

An important part of Oakley's legacy in relation to these discussions of distributional inequality has been her continuing use of the category of women despite criticism that it masks the heterogeneity of the people it locates together. Oakley had been mindful of the implications of class differences for women's experiences of gender oppression as she undertook her studies of housework and becoming a mother, notwithstanding her concerns about allocating a woman a class position based on her husband's occupation. Working-class women's greater vulnerability to death in childbirth offered a particularly stark expression of the consequences of material inequality. In *Housewife*, she also reflected on the women's liberation movement's arguments being perceived as patronising and impractical by women most hard-pressed through material disadvantage. Further dimensions of differences between women also demanded attention. Women from ethnic minorities flagged the distinctive discrimination that they experienced, and similar points were made about lines of division relating to disability, age, nationality, sexual orientation and household type, sometimes noting the cumulative nature of disadvantage; the higher rates of poverty and of lone motherhood among women of Afro-Caribbean heritage illustrated the point. The concept of gender problematised the argument that what women had in common was their biological femaleness, but Oakley rejected the conclusion reached by postmodernists that women's growing awareness of their heterogeneity and their attendant political fragmentation had made the category of women redundant. In her view, cases in which the category of women was deployed to their disadvantage needed to be challenged on this ground. She noted, for example, that women were alleged to be less reliable employees than men because of their higher rate of absence due to sickness and cited Sara Arber's research using quantitative data from the General Household Survey which showed this supposition to be incorrect once the length of absences was taken into account, men's absences from work being typically longer than women's. The broad category of women was also important in the stock-taking exercises that Oakley undertook. These noted, among other things, that the law had changed regarding women's rights in their personal relationships, that women have gained more control over their bodies and that blatant discrimination in the field of employment was no longer tolerated, but they also revealed that such changes in the legal position of women did not constitute the end of patriarchy, merely its capacity to regenerate in new forms.

Feminist responses to the persistence of gender inequality in one form or another were portrayed by some observers as the politics of rage treating men as the enemy, but this was not an accurate characterisation of Oakley's position. Mitchell's argument that women can be more exploratory, expressed as the capacity to move into the future first, led her and Oakley in *What is Feminism?* to highlight how feminist debates involved not only impassioned critiques of the status quo but also alternative visions of social organisation which transcend gender-related conflicts. The flourishing country populated solely by women and girls narrated in Gilman's utopian novel *Herland* was an exercise of imagination with obvious appeal to separatists whose ideal of exclusively female social groups was easy to appreciate in the context of the misogyny that underpinned much of the backlash against feminism. Gilman's description of the steep learning curve of the three male visitors (including a sociologist) to this strange world meant, however, that her message about women's potential to live together peaceably in the absence of familiar gender norms had far-reaching implications for men and masculinity as well. Oakley's own novels employ various plot devices to explore people's efforts to move beyond conflictual gendered relationships, though the pattern is for the central female character to be further along the route to self-awareness than the men in the stories (with Pete Wates in *Scenes Originating in the Garden of Eden* and Nathan Henry in *The strange lockdown life of Alice Henry* being possible exceptions). Oakley has always prized people knowing what they think and being able to articulate this in discussions with others who hold alternative viewpoints. She has argued consistently that women's subordinate position facilitates their development of insights; conversely, men's power constitutes an obstacle to things being seen clearly because prospective gains through escaping masculinity's toxicity via a less-gendered future are complicated by the loss of patriarchal privileges. Concern for the welfare of others captured in the notion of sisterhood and in the practice of caring roles that are predominantly undertaken by women offers one model for people living together more peaceably than a world of masculine competitive individualism, given that there is no reason in principle for altruistic behaviour to be gendered.

Oakley followed her father in reflecting on connections between altruism and public policy, exemplified in the facilitation of blood donation by the National Health Service (NHS) (on which Titmuss's *The Gift Relationship* reported). Along with female enfranchisement in 1918 and 1928 and greater control over fertility brought by the 1967 Abortion Act, Oakley considered the creation of the NHS in the 1940s to be the three most important policy changes in the twentieth century that improved the lives of UK women. The NHS could not relieve women of the whole burden of unpaid caring responsibilities which had proved so restrictive to earlier generations, but it did ameliorate this labour of love. Together with more effective birth control (which dramatically reduced the number of years that the average woman spent either pregnant or lactating), this change facilitated married women's employment. The research participants in Pearl Jephcott's 1962 study regarded mothers taking on paid work as unselfish because the income brought an improved standard of living to all family members. It was altruistic in a less attractive sense where such work was undertaken without housework and childcare tasks being reallocated; these have remained primarily women's responsibility within families, giving unpaid work the character of a second shift, as the American feminist sociologist Arlie Hochschild memorably put it. Oakley's calls in *Housewife* for the abolition of the nuclear family as a prerequisite of a less gendered society treated it as an oppressive institution which isolated women from the practical aid and emotional intelligence of the extensive support networks commonly found in other times and places. This theme was returned to in *Social Support and Motherhood* and rather differently in *The Secret Lives of Eleanor Jenkinson* where the heroine discovers the veracity of Virginia Woolf's observation about women novelists needing a room of their own, away from domestic responsibilities. Family arrangements built around women's self-sacrifice for the benefit of others and the transmission across generations of associated gender ideologies have proved very difficult to dislodge; indeed, they constitute core points of reference in the backlash against feminism. Oakley's early exposure of myths about motherhood involving instinctive altruism and her wider critique of stereotypical family life contrasted the gulf people (including herself) experienced between expectations and realities; love, happiness and fulfilment were difficult to realise fully when tempered by depression, drudgery and the sense of lives going nowhere. Social scientists' messages like this one about altruism's downside relating to the paradox of feeling bad despite doing good are sometimes hard for intended audiences to hear.

Oakley had already encountered the writings of the major sociological figures Talcott Parsons and Mills as an undergraduate and gravitated towards the latter's critique of the former's unduly sanguine perspective on social order. Mills treated conflicts rooted in social structural inequalities as normal, and this perspective was readily extendable to the field of gender inequalities, as was his encouragement to exercise the sociological imagination when considering how things could be different, what Oakley in *Gender on Planet Earth* called world travelling. This latter task was nevertheless daunting because identifying what needed to change to resolve (or at least reduce) gender-related conflict had a long and uneven history. If the lesson of the suffrage movement was that women gaining the vote was a necessary but not a sufficient condition for their liberation, the same was true for legislation dating from the period of second-wave feminism such as laws relating to sex discrimination and equal pay. Similar conclusions could be drawn about the practical campaigns of first-wave feminists to address the hardships and restrictions endured by women that Oakley chronicled in *Women, Peace and Welfare*. Even though only a fraction of the improvements that Jane Addams promoted were realised during her lifetime, she left a legacy of inspirational experimentation for subsequent generations to build on as they sought new ways of living and of understanding the world that extended beyond conventional wisdom. The radical nature of the Nobel Peace Prize winner's pioneering reform initiatives, her involvement in international networks and the range of issues she set about tackling made her the most famous woman in America at the time; critics considered her the most dangerous. Oakley quickly showed her preparedness to follow suit by adopting controversial ideas, for example, when impugning Parsons's characterisation of housework in her first study and in her second when challenging usage of his concept of the sick role to analyse the relationship of patients to doctors. Her championing of randomised controlled trials also showed her capacity to confront accepted ideas, as did the critiques advanced in *Gender on Planet Earth* of psychoanalysis, neoclassical economics, sociobiology and postmodernism, all of which she regarded as variants of delusional thinking. Oakley went on to conclude her book by remarking that living sustainably with each other and the planet's ecosystem requires rigorous scrutiny of even the most cherished myths, especially those relating to gender.

Oakley's broad interests in issues of identity and inequality and in political responses (both personal and policy-related) to them raised profound methodological questions about knowledge and truth. She contested the myth of motherhood because it idealised a complex and sometimes ambivalent state; a one-sided focus on having children as a route to fulfilment and contentment gave no warning to prospective parents of the potential difficulties lying ahead. Her interviews with new mothers confirmed that her own experience of motherhood bringing isolation and depression alongside positive emotions was normal. Furthermore, Oakley's exploration in *Taking it like a Woman* of domestic relationships noted that the public face that people present may conceal secrets that are at odds with the myth of happy families. A similar theme runs through *Father and Daughter* where her account of Titmuss's private life was not always consistent with his saintly public profile, thereby exposing it as another type of myth. These and the further myths of the division of labour by sex being natural (traceable back to the story of Adam and Eve in the Garden of Eden, as Oakley discussed in *Sex, Gender and Society*, *Telling the Truth about Jerusalem* and elsewhere in her writings) and of the perfect body (as discussed in *Fracture*) are used by her to urge caution when encountering familiar narratives handed down the generations. Myths have an understandable appeal because they combine grains of truth with nostalgic fictions, but they can be dangerously misleading and warrant examination from different vantage points. Interviewees' accounts featured prominently in what Oakley wrote about housework and motherhood because of her sense that malestream sociology marginalised or distorted these women's points of view, leading her to conclude that there is never only one truth. The argument in *Forgotten Wives* about the partiality of historians' focus on famous men also pointed to this conclusion regarding the gendered character of knowledge. Her more general argument made in *Experiments in Knowing* was that there is a long history of the credibility given to ideas varying according to the social standing of the person putting them forward. The sociologist Trent Lovett, a character in her novel *Overheads*, also cast doubt on the idea of knowledge ever being straightforward, in the process illustrating Oakley's point that understanding the world can come through various routes, fiction as well as non-fiction.

Oakley's response to the existence of different ways of knowing was not to treat them as equally credible but rather to seek to discriminate between them by paying attention to the nature of the competing knowledge claims being advanced, with a particular focus on their methodological foundations. In *The Sociology of Housework*, her objections to malestream sociology concerned its predominant focus on men and corresponding neglect of women (which can be regarded as a sampling issue) and its misrepresentation of women when they were discussed (which was at least in part a result of over-reliance on theoretical reasoning rather than on the analysis of empirical evidence). By the 1980s, she had become embroiled (reluctantly) in the paradigm wars being waged between rival supporters of qualitative and quantitative methods whose treatment of the issue as one of diametrical opposites she found problematic, preferring instead to make the case for methodological pluralism which included the use of mixed methods where appropriate. She was unconvinced by the argument that by its nature, feminist research had a closer affinity to qualitative methods than it did to quantitative ones and feared that such claims made it easier for feminist sociologists to be marginalised. Her study of social support and motherhood may not have entirely allayed her audience's concerns about using the particular techniques of randomised controlled trials but the more general effect of her work has been to help to persuade many researchers (including feminists) of the value of quantification for many tasks. This is particularly the case for policy-related research where the use of statistical data assists in identifying the success or otherwise of policy interventions, sometimes as part of a mixed methods approach. Oakley's establishment of the Social Science Research Unit in 1990 was associated with her growing engagement in the fields of

evaluation and systematic reviewing, where once again shortcomings in research design, the presence of erratic procedures in
data collection and analysis and researchers' failure to present
sufficient information about their studies for them to be properly
evaluated were all frequent matters of concern for her and her
colleagues. Oakley's subsequent return to the study of archival
material in her work on the buried history of women's contributions to the development of social science also involved
reflection on the most appropriate way of proceeding methodologically. She had particular ethical concerns about the idea that
documents are there to be plundered by researchers irrespective
of the wishes of people now deceased whose material is being
analysed.

Pioneers of new ways of working must expect to meet resis-
tance from researchers wedded to their own preferred practice,
and in making the case for change, Oakley regularly prompted
controversy. She shared Mills's misgivings about analyses that
were constructed around grand theory but in turn found her
work criticised from various quarters as insufficiently theoretical.
Bob Mullan's 1980s interview with her provided an opportunity
to respond to such criticism by expressing scepticism regarding
the practice of using theory in a way that was detached from
engaging with real-world problems; she treated this as theorising
for theory's sake. Oakley reiterated her preference for grounding
theory in empirical research often in subsequent decades, during
which time the case for researchers' work being judged by its
potential applications and impact on people's lives as well as its
intellectual rigour has become much more widely accepted.
Another controversy relates to Oakley's preparedness to break
new ground methodologically, illustrated by her inclusion of a
randomised controlled trial among the methods used to study
social support and motherhood. She had become familiar with
this method thanks to the epidemiologist Iain Chalmers; their
cross-disciplinary collaboration demonstrated the potential of

dialogue between practitioners of medical and social sciences. Her association with Chalmers's National Perinatal Epidemiological Unit saw her not only add experimental methods to her repertoire but also elaborate on her case for medical professionals taking more seriously women's points of view that had been captured in qualitative interviews and ethnographic observation. Oakley's ability to work across academic boundaries was apparent as well in her long-standing collaborative writing projects on feminism with her co-editor Mitchell despite being unconvinced by her psychoanalytical perspective. The argument advanced in *Subject Women* that women's studies offered much from which men might learn likewise revealed a preparedness to engage with people starting out from fundamentally different positions provided that they approached such dialogues with open-mindedness. She was, however, under no illusions about the backward-looking character of the backlash against second-wave feminism that was building momentum at that time, about which she was uncompromising. A rather different type of controversy was generated by Oakley's experimentation with modes of presenting her ideas that went beyond standard academic practice, such as her inclusion of poems in *Telling the Truth about Jerusalem* and the unconventional forms of authorship deployed in *Gender on Planet Earth* for which the world may not yet be ready, she concluded.

Women who engage with controversial issues risk being labelled difficult, as *A Critical Woman* and *Women, Peace and Welfare* illustrated. Chafing at rules and norms that treated women as outsiders in a man-made world was an important spur to action for Oakley just as it had been for Addams, Gilman, Woolf, de Beauvoir, Wootton, Friedan, Jephcott and the many other predecessors from whose efforts to challenge gender inequality and related social problems she drew inspiration. Oakley continued to be controversial in maturity as in youth. In *Gender on Planet Earth*, for example, she advanced a reformulation of the main problem facing contemporary societies, identifying this not so much as gender inequality but rather as the harmful effects that the institutionalised system of gender has on everyone (men as well as women) and everything from the state of the planet to what counts as knowledge. As a result, she argued, there is a pressing need to work across deeply ingrained divides to fashion a more sustainable future in which gender differences play a diminishing role. Researchers may find themselves better known for ideas expounded earlier in their careers than those that have had less time to be taken up and discussed widely, and that is currently true in Oakley's case. In terms of citations, she continues to have most recognition for her early work on gender, housework and the practice of interviewing. Such profiles are nevertheless constantly evolving. Her greater engagement with systematic reviewing and with policy evaluation are among her interests that developed in mid-career that have grown in importance alongside these older elements of her output, as have her historical investigations into women's contributions to nascent social science. The substantive issues that will in the future feature most prominently in her legacy could conceivably relate to any of the broad questions of identity, inequality, solidarity or knowledge-making which this chapter has identified as central to her work. Whatever transpires, her enduring influence will bear the hallmarks of careful detective work that is driven by inquisitiveness about the curious and complex character of people's lives, the methodological rigour required to make sense of how these lives come to be patterned as they are and, crucially, the imagination to envisage how lives could be improved and how such potential futures might be brought about.

APPENDIX 1: ANN OAKLEY'S PUBLICATIONS

This appendix lists Oakley's main publications, both authored and co-authored, in chronological order. The reference numbers O1–O81 are those used in appendix 2 to show the relationship to this book. A full list of her publications is available as part of her CV on her website http://www.annoakley.co.uk/index.html along with other material about her.

1970

O1 The myth of motherhood. *New Society*, 26 February, 348–350.

1972

O2 *Sex, Gender and Society*. London: Temple Smith. (new editions 1985, 2015.)

1974

O3 *Housewife*. London: Allen Lane.

O4 *The Sociology of Housework*. London: Martin Robertson. (new editions 1985, 2019.)

1976

O5 Mitchell J, Oakley A (eds) *The Rights and Wrongs of Women*. Harmondsworth: Penguin.

1979

O6 *Becoming a Mother*. Oxford: Martin Robertson. (republished as *From Here to Maternity* 1981, 1986, 2019.)

O7 Oakley A, Oakley R 'Sexism in official statistics' in Irvine J, Miles I, Evans J (eds) *Demystifying Social Statistics*. London: Pluto Press, pp. 172–189.

1980

O8 *Women Confined: Towards a Sociology of Childbirth*. Oxford: Martin Robertson. (new edition 1986.)

1981

O9 *Subject Women*. Oxford: Martin Robertson.

O10 Graham H, Oakley A 'Competing ideologies of reproduction: medical and maternal perspectives on pregnancy and birth' in Roberts H (ed.) *Women, Health and Reproduction*. London: Routledge and Kegan Paul, pp. 50–74.

O11 'Interviewing women: a contradiction in terms?' in Roberts H (ed.) *Doing Feminist Research*. London: Routledge and Kegan Paul, pp. 30–61.

1982

O12 Oakley A, Chalmers I, Macfarlane JA 'Social class, stress and reproduction' in Rees A R, Purcell H (eds) *Disease and the Environment*. Chichester: John Wiley, pp. 11–50.

O13 'Normal motherhood: an exercise in self-control?' in Hutter B, Williams G (eds) *Controlling Women*. London: Croom Helm, pp. 79–107.

O14 'Conventional families' in Rapoport R N, Rapoport R, Fogarty M P (eds) *Families in Britain*. London: Routledge and Kegan Paul, pp. 123–137.

1983

O15 'Women and health policy' in Lewis J (ed.) *Women's Welfare, Women's Rights*. London: Croom Helm, pp. 103–129.

O16 'Millicent Garrett Fawcett' in Spender D (ed.) *Feminist Theorists*. London: The Women's Press, pp. 184–202.

1984

O17 Oakley A, McPherson A, Roberts H *Miscarriage*. London: Fontana. (new edition 1990.)

O18 *The Captured Womb: A History of the Medical Care of Pregnant Women*. Oxford: Basil Blackwell.

O19 *Taking it Like a Woman*. London: Jonathan Cape.

1986

O20 Mitchell J, Oakley A (eds) *What is Feminism?* Oxford: Basil Blackwell.

O21 *Telling the Truth About Jerusalem: A Collection of Essays and Poems*. Oxford: Basil Blackwell.

1988

O22 *The Men's Room*. London: Virago.

1989

O23 'Simone de Beauvoir' in Forster P, Sutton I (eds) *Daughters of de Beauvoir*. London: The Women's Press, pp. 67–76.

O24 'Women's studies in British sociology: to end at our beginning?' *British Journal of Sociology* 40 (3), pp. 442–470.

O25 'Smoking in pregnancy: smokescreen or risk factor? Towards a materialist analysis' *Sociology of Health and Illness* 11 (4), pp. 311–335.

O26 'Who's afraid of the randomized controlled trial? Some dilemmas of the scientific method and "good" research practice' *Women and Health* 15 (2), pp. 25–59.

1990

O27 Oakley A, Houd S *Helpers in Childbirth: Midwifery Today*. Washington, DC: Hemisphere Books, on behalf of the World Health Organization.

O28 Oakley A, Rajan L 'Social class and social support: the same or different?' *Sociology* 25 (1), pp. 31–59.

O29 Oakley A, Rajan L, Grant A 'Social support and pregnancy outcome' *British Journal of Obstetrics and Gynaecology* 97, pp. 155–162.

O30 (under the name Rosamund Clay) *Only Angels Forget*. London: Virago.

1991

O31 'Eugenics, social medicine and the career of Richard Titmuss in Britain 1935-50' *British Journal of Sociology* 42 (2), pp. 165–194.

O32 Elbourne D, Oakley A 'An overview of trials of social support during pregnancy: effects on gestational age at delivery and birthweight' in Berendes H W, Kessel W, Yaffe S (eds) *Prevention of Low Birthweight*. Washington DC: National Centre for Education in Maternal and Child Health, pp. 205–223.

O33 *Matilda's Mistake*. London: Virago.

1992

O34 *Social Support and Motherhood: The Natural History of a Research Project*. Oxford: Basil Blackwell. (new edition 2019).

O35 *The Secret Lives of Eleanor Jenkinson*. London: HarperCollins.

1993

O36 *Essays on Women, Medicine and Health*. Edinburgh: Edinburgh University Press.

O37 *Scenes Originating in the Garden of Eden*. London: HarperCollins.

1994

O38 Brannen J, Dodd K, Oakley A, Storey P *Young People, Health and Family Life*. Buckingham: Open University Press.

O39 Oakley A, Williams AS (eds) *The Politics of the Welfare State*. London: UCL Press.

1995

O40 Fullerton D, Holland J, Oakley A 'Towards effective intervention: evaluating HIV prevention and sexual health education' in Aggleton P, Davies P, Hart G (eds) *AIDS: Safety, Sexuality and Risk*. London: Taylor and Francis, pp. 90–108.

1996

O41 *Man and Wife: Richard and Kay Titmuss, My Parents' Early Years*. London: HarperCollins.

O42 *A Proper Holiday*. London: HarperCollins.

1997

O43 Oakley A, Mitchell J (eds) *Who's Afraid of Feminism?* London: Hamish Hamilton.

O44 Oakley A, Ashton J (eds) *The Gift Relationship: From Human Blood to Social Policy*. By Richard M Titmuss. London: LSE Books.

1998

O45 Williams F, Popay J, Oakley A (eds) *Welfare Research: A Critical Review*. London: UCL Press.

O46 Oakley A, Rigby A S 'Are men good for the welfare of women and children?' in Popay J, Hearn J, Edwards J (eds) *Men, Gender Divisions and Welfare*. London: Routledge, pp. 101–127.

O47 'Science, gender and women's liberation: an argument against postmodernism' *Women's Studies International Forum* 21 (2), pp. 133–146.

O48 'Gender, methodology and people's ways of knowing: some problems with feminism and the paradigm debate in social science' *Sociology* 32 (4), pp. 707–731.

1999

O49 *Overheads*. London: HarperCollins.

2000

O50 *Experiments in Knowing: Gender and Method in the Social Sciences*. Cambridge: Polity Press.

O51 'Paradigm wars: some thoughts on a personal and public trajectory' *International Journal of Social Research Methodology* 2 (3), pp. 247–254.

2001

O52 Alcock P, Glennerster H, Oakley A, Sinfield A (eds) *Welfare and Wellbeing: Richard Titmuss's Contribution to Social Policy*. Bristol: Policy Press.

O53 'Evaluating health promotion: methodological diversity' in Oliver S, Peersman G (eds) *Using Research for Effective Health Promotion*. Buckingham: Open University Press, pp. 16–31.

054 Peersman G, Oliver S, Oakley A 'Systematic reviews of effectiveness' in Oliver S, Peersman G (eds) *Using Research for Effective Health Promotion*. Buckingham: Open University Press, pp. 96–108.

O55 Oliver S, Peersman G, Oakley A, Nicholas A 'Using research: challenges in evidence informed service planning' in Oliver S, Peersman G (eds) *Using Research for Effective Health Promotion*. Buckingham: Open University Press, pp. 96–108.

O56 Strange V, Forrest S, Oakley A 'A listening trial: 'qualitative' methods within experimental research' in Oliver S, Peersman G (eds) *Using Research for Effective Health Promotion*. Buckingham: Open University Press, pp. 138–153.

2002

O57 *Gender on Planet Earth*. Cambridge: Polity Press.

O58 'Social science and evidence-based everything: the case of education' *Educational Review* 54 (3), pp. 277–286.

2003

O59 Oakley A, Strange V, Toroyan T, Wiggins M, Roberts I, Stephenson J 'Using random allocation to evaluate social interventions: three recent UK examples' *Annals of the American Academy of Political and Social Science* 589 (1), pp. 170–189.

2004

O60 Oakley A, Barker J (eds) *Private Complaints and Public Health: Richard Titmuss on the National Health Service.* Bristol: Policy Press.

O61 'Epilogue in Eight Essays: Ann Oakley' in Halsey A H (ed.) *A History of Sociology in Britain: Science, Literature and Society.* Oxford: Oxford University Press, pp. 214–217.

2005

O62 *The Ann Oakley Reader: Gender, Women and Social Science.* Bristol: Policy Press.

O63 Oliver S, Harden A, Rees R, Shepherd J, Brunton G, Garcia J, Oakley A 'An emerging framework for including different types of evidence in systematic reviews for public policy' *Evaluation* 11 (4), pp. 428–446.

O64 Oakley A, Gough D, Oliver S, Thomas J 'The politics of evidence and methodology: lessons from the EPPI-Centre' *Evidence and Policy* 1 (1), pp. 5–31.

2006

O65 Oakley A, Strange V, Bonell C, Allen E, Stephenson J 'Process evaluation in randomised controlled trials of complex interventions' *British Medical Journal* 332, pp. 413–416.

2007

O66 *Fracture: Adventures of a Broken Body.* Bristol: Policy Press.

2010

O67 'The social science of biographical life-writing: some methodological and ethical issues' *International Journal of Social Research Methodology* 13(5), pp. 425–439.

2011

O68 *A Critical Woman: Barbara Wootton, Social Science and Public Policy in the Twentieth Century*. London: Bloomsbury Academic.

O69 Oakley A, Wiggins M, Strange V, Sawtell M, Austerberry H 'Becoming a mother: continuities and discontinuities over three decades' in Ebtehaj F, Herring J, Johnson MH, Richards M (eds) *Birth Rights and Rites*. Oxford, Hart Publishing, pp. 9–27.

2012

O70 'The strange case of the two Wootton Reports: what can we learn about the evidence policy relationship?' *Evidence & Policy* 8(3), pp. 267–283.

2014

O71 *Father and Daughter: Patriarchy, Gender and Social Science*. Bristol: Policy Press.

2015

O72 'Imagining social science' in Twamley K, Doidge M, Scott A (eds) *Sociologists' Tales: Contemporary Narratives on Sociological Thought and Practice*. Bristol: Policy Press, pp. 109–116.

O73 'The history of gendered social science: a personal narrative and some reflections on method' *Women's History Review* 24 (2), pp. 154–173.

2016

O74 'Interviewing women again: power, time and the gift' *Sociology* 50 (1), pp. 195–213.

O75 'The sociology of childbirth: an autobiographical journey through four decades of research' *Sociology of Health and Illness* 38 (5), pp. 689–705.

2018

O76 *Women, Peace and Welfare: A Suppressed History of Social Reform, 1880–1920*. Bristol: Policy Press.

2019

O77 'Legacies of altruism: Richard Titmuss, Marie Meinhardt, and health policy research in the 1940s' *Social Policy & Society* 18(3), pp. 383–392.

2020

O78 'Women, the early development of sociological research methods in Britain and the London School of Economics: A (partially) retrieved history' *Sociology* 54 (2), pp. 292–331.

2021

O79 *Forgotten Wives: How Women Get Written Out of History*. Bristol: Policy Press.

2022

O80 *The Strange Lockdown Life of Alice Henry*. London: Linen Press.

2024

O81 *The Science of Housework*. Bristol: Policy Press.

APPENDIX 2: SOURCES AND FURTHER READING

This appendix gives the principal original sources for each chapter, using the cross-references listed in appendix 1. Other material is included as the basis for further reading.

Chapter 1 Oakley's reflections on how her life has been shaped by its social and historical context can be found in O19 (published when she was 40) and O71 (published three decades later). Chapter 11 of Dale Spender's *For the Record* (London: The Women's Press, 1985) locates Oakley as a key developer of feminist ideas inspired by Betty Friedan, while Margaret Walters' *Feminism: A Very Short Introduction* (Oxford: Oxford University Press, 2005) traces feminist ideas across several centuries down to second wave feminists including Oakley. (Oakley herself prefers not to apply the imagery of waves to feminism's history.) Olive Banks' *Faces of Feminism* (Oxford: Blackwell, 1986) covers similar ground but starts in the 1840s, as does Sara Delamont's *Feminist Sociology* (London: SAGE, 2003) (although she calls the period from the 1960s feminism's *third* wave). Miriam David's *Reclaiming Feminism* (Bristol: Policy Press, 2016) covers more recent developments down to fifth wave feminism, drawing on her own career as a contemporary of Oakley's. Julia Brannen's *Social Research Matters* (Bristol: Bristol University Press, 2019) is a more straightforwardly autobiographical account by another academic contemporary and Institute of Education colleague. Sheila Rowbotham's *A Century of Women* (London: Penguin, 1999) devotes a chapter to each decade of the 20th century, focusing on Britain and the USA, describing the 1960s as a decade of ferment.

Chapter 2 Beyond Oakley's main autobiographical/ semi-autobiographical books O19 and O71 she provides insights into her life and career in further places including articles on particular topics such as O51, O73 and O75, her contextualisation of the material selected for O21, O36 and O62 and her career reflections in O61 and O72. Gabriela Loureiro's 2021 interview, 'Feminist histories, feminist futures', discusses Oakley's involvement in the Women's Liberation Movement in Ealing   https://autonomy.work/portfolio/ffp-ann-oakley-int/ Chapter 9 of Graham Crow's *The Art of Sociological Argument* (Basingstoke: Palgrave, 2005) treats Oakley as successor to various sociological predecessors, notably Charles Wright Mills, while his 'Hedgehogs, foxes and other embodiments of academics' career trajectories' in *Contemporary Social Science* 2020 vol. 15 (5) pp. 577–594 considers her career trajectory and his contribution on Oakley in Atkinson P, Delamont S, Cernat A, Sakshaug JW, Williams RA (eds) *The Sage Encyclopaedia of Research Methods* (London: SAGE, 2021) focuses on her research methods, as does Lucinda Platt's contribution to *50 Key Sociologists* (edited by John Scott, Routledge, Abingdon, 2007).

Chapter 3 Oakley's first article O1 and her book on gender O2, her books on housework O3 and O4 and her books and chapters on her first two research projects on motherhood O5, O6, O8, O10, O13 and O18 are the principal sources used in this chapter. The literature on gender has grown to vast proportions, as Oakley notes in the introduction to the 2015 edition of O2. Pamela Abbott's chapter in Geoff Payne and Eric Harrison's edited collection *Social Divisions* (4th edition

Bristol: Policy Press, 2020) considers the range of gender inequalities. Kath Woodward's *The short guide to gender* (Bristol: Policy Press, 2011) provides a useful overview of how debates about gender developed. Momin Rahman and Stevi Jackson's *Gender and Sexuality* (Cambridge: Polity Press, 2010) is a similarly useful introduction to this topic. Stevi Jackson and Sue Scott's edited collection *Gender: A sociological reader* (London: Routledge, 2002) contains 50 chapters that reveal how broadly the concept was being applied by the turn of the century, including in the field of paid and unpaid work which Oakley's research on housework had also stimulated. In her introduction to the 2019 edition of O4 she suggests that this is her most influential book and reflects on the course of the debates that followed its publication in 1974, including the point that some contributions were more methodologically sophisticated without being more illuminating as a result. The book's success came despite the hostility of some reviewers such as Dorothy Smith who was among the contributors to a review symposium in *Sociology* 1975 vol. 9 (3), pp. 515–524, and others mentioned in Oakley's new preface to the 1985 edition. Oakley's introduction to the 2019 edition of O6, her first book on motherhood, includes a discussion of the mixed reviews that it received, including in popular as well as academic publications. Researchers since the 1970s (when Oakley conducted her original study of motherhood) have highlighted the growing diversity of family forms and household types in which mothers are found; Oakley herself does this in her re-study O69, as do Deborah Chambers and Pablo Gracia in *Sociology of Family Life* (Cambridge: Polity Press, 2021).

Chapter 4 Oakley's concerns with women's well-being, with policy initiatives to promote it and with the methodological challenges of researching these issues feature prominently in the publications on which this chapter draws, notably O7, O9, O11, O12, O14, O15, O17, O24, O25, O26, O27, O28,

O29, O32, O34, O38, O48 and O51. The distinctiveness of the field of women's studies was debated in two edited collections, Dale Spender's *Men's Studies Modified* (Oxford: Pergamon Press, 1981) and Gloria Bowles and Renate Duelli Klein's *Theories of Women's Studies* (London: Routledge and Kegan Paul, 1983). Two edited collections, Mary Evans' *The Woman Question* (London: SAGE, 1994) and Sandra Kemp and Judith Squires' *Feminisms* (Oxford: Oxford University Press, 1997), took stock of things a decade on. Gayle Letherby's *Feminist Research in Theory and Practice* (Buckingham: Open University Press, 2003) included discussion of the quantitative/qualitative divide in research methods. Alan Bryman's 'The end of the paradigm wars?' in Pertti Alasuutari, Leonard Bickman and Julia Brannen (eds) *The Sage Handbook of Social Research Methods* (London: SAGE, 2008, pp. 13–25) provides a useful review of the issues over which these methodological disputes raged, written from a non-partisan position. Vicki Plano Clark and John Cresswell's co-edited *The Mixed Methods Reader* (Thousand Oaks, California: SAGE, 2008) considers the paradigm wars among many other topics.

Chapter 5 This chapter draws on Oakley's writings about evaluation in the broad sense including discussions of the conduct of robust social science (O53, O54, O55, O56, O58, O59, O63, O64 and O65) and of implications for policy (O39, O40, O45 and O46) together with reflections about the legacy of Titmuss's work (O31, O44, O52 and O60) and the cumulative nature of knowledge more generally (O20, O43, O47, O50, O62, O69 and 073). The web pages of the Social Science Research Unit https://www.ucl.ac.uk/ioe/departments-and-centres/centres/social-science-research-unit-ssru and of the EPPI Centre https://eppi.ioe.ac.uk/cms/ provide details of the extensive work undertaken there in the last three decades. Sandy Oliver's 'Ann Oakley: new learning and global influence from working across conventional boundaries' *London Review of*

Education 2023, 21 (1) is a review of Oakley's work in evaluation by a key colleague. David Byrne's *Applying Social Science* (Bristol: Policy Press, 2011) has a useful chapter on evaluation research which includes discussion of the experiments seeking to break the cycle of deprivation with which Halsey had been involved. John Stewart's *Richard Titmuss: A Commitment to Welfare* (Bristol: Policy Press, 2020) is an authoritative biography on which Oakley collaborated.

Chapter 6 Oakley's in-depth historical biographical research is exemplified in book-length studies O41, O68, O71, O76, O79 and O81 and in shorter chapters and articles O16, O23, O67, O70, O73, O75, O77 and O78. Barbara Wootton's *In a World I Never Made* (London: George Allen and Unwin, 1967) is (like all autobiographies) a selective account, published more than two decades before her death. Charlotte Perkins Gilman's *The Home: Its Work and Influence* (Lanham: AltaMira Press, 2002) has an introduction to this 1903 classic that treats it as a forerunner of Betty Friedan's work. Because the LSE figured frequently in the lives of the women on whom Oakley's historical research has focused, Christopher Husbands' *Sociology at the London School of Economics and Political Science 1904–2015* (Cham: Palgrave Macmillan, 2019) provides much useful contextual information, as does John Scott's broader *British Sociology: A History* (Cham: Palgrave Pivot, 2020). Lynn McDonald's *The Women Founders of the Social Sciences* (Ottawa: Carleton University Press, 1994) covers an earlier period.

Chapter 7 Oakley's autobiographical reflections along with more general observations can be found in O19, O57, O66, O71, O72 and O75 and in interviews conducted by Bob Mullan in Mullan B (ed.) *Sociologists on Sociology*, London: Croom Helm, 1987 and by Liz Spencer for the UK Data Service Pioneers of Qualitative Research project which is available at http://ukdataservice.ac.uk/teaching-resources/pioneers and which is

drawn upon in Paul Thompson, Ken Plummer and Neli Dem-
ireva's *Pioneering Social Research: Life Stories of a Generation*,
Bristol: Policy Press, 2021. O71 has a review symposium
devoted to it in *Sociology* 51(2) 2017, pp. 483–490 and a
response from Oakley. 'Writing fiction as a sociologist: an
interview with Ann Oakley' *The Sociological Review Magazine*
March 29 2019 https://thesociologicalreview.org/collections/
sociology-and-literature/writing-fiction-as-a-sociologist-an-inter-
view-with-ann-oakley/ focuses on novel writing. Oakley's novels
are O22, O30, O33, O35, O37, O42, O49 and O80; they are
discussed in Alla Marchyshyna and Anatolii Skrypnyk, 'Feminine identities in Ann Oakley's novels' *Journal of European
Studies* 2021, 51 (2), pp. 129–138. 'In conversation with Ann
Oakley' is a discussion of methodological issues https://
www.ncrm.ac.uk/resources/video/RMF2010/pages/Wednesday.
php from 2010.

Chapter 8 Barbara Littlewood's *Feminist Perspectives on
Sociology* (London: Routledge, 2004) gives a sense of how
much the discipline changed during Oakley's career, providing
one way of thinking about her legacy. Barbara Laslett and
Barrie Thorne's edited collection *Feminist Sociology: Life
Histories of a Movement* (New Jersey: Rutgers University
Press, 1997) provides an interesting comparison with American autobiographical reflections. A. Javier Trevino's *The
Emerald Guide to C. Wright Mills* (Bingley: Emerald, 2021)
facilitates reflection on Oakley's acknowledged debt to Mills's
ideas and how she built on them.

INDEX

.

Printed in the USA
CPSIA information can be obtained
at www.ICGtesting.com
JSHW012133280524
63817JS00003B/3